FIRST STEPS IN STARTING A FOUNDATION

Fourth Edition

JOHN A. EDIE

STATEMENT OF INCLUSIVENESS

The Council on Foundations was formed to promote responsible and effective philanthropy. This mission requires a commitment to inclusiveness as a fundamental operating principle and calls for an active and ongoing process which affirms human diversity in its many forms, encompassing but not limited to ethnicity, race, gender, sexual orientation, economic circumstance, disability, and philosophy. We seek diversity in order to ensure that a range of perspectives, opinions, and experiences are recognized and acted upon in achieving the Council's mission. The Council also asks members to make a similar commitment to inclusiveness in order to better enhance their abilities to contribute to the common good of our changing society.

©1997 Council on Foundations, Inc.
All rights reserved.

COUNCIL ON FOUNDATIONS
1828 L Street, N.W.
Washington, DC 20036
202.466.6512

Printed on recycled paper.

Contents

Preface v

Part One: Introduction 1

Part Two: Public v. Private 5

Definition of a Private Foundation 6
The Concept of Publicness 8
    Exception 1: Traditional Charities and Publicly Supported Organization #1 8
    Exception 2: Gross Receipts Charities or Publicly Supported Organization #2 11
    Exception 3: Supporting Organization 12
Public v. Private: Effect on the Living Donor 14
    Percentage Limits on Gifts of Cash 14
    Percentage Limits on Gifts of Appreciated Property .. 14
    Five-Year Carryover 15
    Limits on Value of gifts of Appreciated Property 15
Public v. Private: Effect on the Organization 17
    Two Percent Excise Tax on Investment Income (Section 4940) 17
    Tax on Acts of Self-Dealing (Section 4941) 17
    Tax on Failure to Meet Minimum Distribution (Section 4942) 18
    Tax on Excess Business Holdings (Section 4943) 18
    Tax on Jeopardy Investments (Section 4944) 19
    Tax on Taxable Expenditures (Section 4945) 19
    Regulatory Scheme for Public Charities—1996 Intermediate Sanctions 21
    Reporting Requirements (Section 6033) 22
Summary of Part Two 23

Part Three: What Is a Private Foundation? 25

General Use of the Term Foundation 26
    Independent Foundation 27
    Company Foundation 27
    Conduit or Pass-through Foundation 28
    Pooled Common Funds 28
    Operating Foundation 29
    Exempt Operating Foundation 32

Part Four: The Community Foundation Option 35

Developers of a Capital Pool for Philanthropy 36
Distributors of Funds for Philanthropy 36
Form 36
Geography and Size 37

Part Four: The Community Foundation Option (cont'd)
Governing Body 37
Range of Service to Donors 37
Variance Power 38

Part Five: Choosing the Right Type of Foundation 39
A Word About Size 39
The Public Charity (or Public Foundation) Options 40
    The Traditional Charity—Section 509(a)(1) 41
    The Gross Receipts Charity—Section 509(a)(2) 41
    The Supporting Organization—Section 509 (a)(3) 42
    The Community Foundation 43
The Private Foundation Options 44
    The Independent Foundation 44
    The Company-Sponsored Foundation 45
    The Conduit or Pass-Through Foundation 46
    The Pooled Common Fund 47
    The Operating Foundation 48
    The Exempt Operating Foundation 48

Part Six: First Steps in Starting a Foundation 51
Trust or Corporation? 51
    The Trust Option 52
    The Corporate Option 52
    Other Considerations 53
Tax-Exempt Status: State Level 53
    The Trust Agreement 55
    Corporate Documents 55
Tax-Exempt Status: Federal Level 56
    Final v. Advance Rulings 57
    Cumulative List (Publication 78) 58
    Other Federal Requirements 58
Postscript 60

List of References 61

Appendices 73
Sample Articles of Incorporation 73
Sample Bylaws 77
Sample Trust Agreement 86
Council on Foundations Principles and Practices For Effective Grantmaking 93
IRS Form 1023 and Instructions 97

PREFACE

The mission of the Council on Foundations is to serve the public good "by promoting and enhancing responsible and effective philanthropy."

For many years, one of the Council's primary goals has been to encourage the growth of organized grantmaking. More specifically, this goal entails informing potential donors and their professional advisors of the advantages of private, family, corporate and community foundations for organized giving.

We have committed the resources of the Council on Foundations to this endeavor. If philanthropy is to maintain its degree of influence in relation to the growth of the economy and the changing charitable needs of the country, more foundations need to be formed and existing grantmaking foundations need to grow.

This publication, *First Steps in Starting a Foundation*, has helped thousands of donors get an informed headstart in their philanthropic efforts since the first edition 1987. We are pleased to present this updated fourth edition of *First Steps* so that it may continue to serve donors and their advisors as a basic tool in understanding the many grantmaking options available.

Thousands of copies of *First Steps* have been sold to date and it remains an annual bestseller in the Council's list of publications. Literally, hundreds of calls and letters come into our office each year from those who seek just the kind of information and detail *First Steps* provides.

Anyone who has braved the waters of the federal tax code knows how complex and difficult it can be. The study of tax exempt organizations is no exception. Since joining the Council in May of 1981, Senior Vice President and General Counsel John Edie has developed a thorough understanding of this legal specialty. Moreover, through his many writings and numerous speaking engagements, he has translated the arcane tax code into simple, understandable language, as evidenced by this publication. While *First Steps* is not light reading, it does provide the essential introduction to foundations and the tax code necessary for establishing a sound beginning. With 10 years of successful service on its record, I am confident this newly revised fourth edition will continue to provide a valuable introduction to organized philanthropy in its legal context for many years to come.

Dorothy S. Ridings
President and CEO
October, 1997

 # PART ONE

Introduction

Starting a foundation means different things to different people. And not surprisingly, one can create several different types of foundations. In the field of philanthropy, the term foundation has no precise meaning. However, when creating a foundation, nearly everyone is seeking two tax advantages: they want the organization to be tax exempt and they want donors to the organization to treat their donations as tax deductible contributions. To obtain these valuable advantages, the creators of foundations must become familiar with the Internal Revenue Code and state laws that govern the formation and regulate the activities of foundations.

The term foundation is used broadly, as illustrated by these two examples:

Foundation A is formed by a group of concerned citizens to purchase, operate and maintain a small wildlife preserve and county park. The foundation has no endowment and must rely on regular fundraising drives and admission fees to operate the preserve. It makes no grants of any kind. Responsibility for running the foundation is in the hands of a large public board of directors broadly representative of the county.

Foundation B is formed by a wealthy donor to assist in the preservation of wildlife and endangered species in the western United States. In establishing the foundation, the donor makes one large contribution to form an endowment. The sole purpose of the foundation is grantmaking. The foundation does not operate programs or raise funds; rather it makes grants and pays expenses solely from the endowment's investment income. Control of the foundation lies completely in the hands of the donor who chooses the other members of the small board of directors.

Both organizations in the examples just described may be called foundations, yet the differences between their operations are dramatic. More importantly, the application of the tax laws to these two foundations varies substantially.

While general use of the term foundation may not be precise, the tax code definition of "private foundation" is quite specific. When starting a foundation, it is essential for the donor or the donor's adviser to comprehend—at the outset—the basic legal rules. The main purpose of *First Steps* is to help the reader understand the legal framework under which all foundations must operate.

This book is aimed at the grantmaker, not the grantseeker. An important part of the mission of the Council on Foundations is to promote the growth of responsible and effective philanthropy. Therefore, it is hoped this book will stimulate the formation of new grantmaking organizations. The person seeking advice on how to raise funds or how to form a fundraising foundation should note the appropriate section in the list of references.

This book is written for the layman. It is intended as a conceptual discussion, not a legal checklist. Nevertheless, lawyers unfamiliar with the world of exempt organization law may find it useful for an understanding of the legal framework necessary to establish a foundation. While the book provides a basic summary of steps necessary to establish a foundation, the minimum requirements vary from state to state; no attempt is made here to be comprehensive from a strict legal standpoint. Instead, the aim is to introduce the layperson to the rudiments of foundation law so that he or she will have the necessary understanding to move forward.

A word about lawyers: retaining legal counsel normally involves a fee unless you are fortunate enough to have an attorney willing to do the work for free (pro bono). However, whether for free or for fee, it is vital to choose good legal counsel to set up your foundation. After reading this book, it should be clear how complicated the law can be, and, therefore, how essential it is to establish the right type of foundation in the right way. In pursuing this goal, there is no substitute for good legal advice.

Finally, this book is aimed to help the reader save on legal fees. In most circumstances, attorneys will bill for the hours necessary to provide the services needed. By reading and understanding this book, the reader will avoid the time needed for the lawyer to educate him or her on the basics and will narrow the range of issues that the lawyer will need to consider. Also, by understanding the legal framework, the reader will be better able to assist counsel in preparing many of the legal documents necessary to establish the foundation.

Most readers will not know in advance what type of foundation is most appropriate for them. In fact, many will not even know what are their choices. After reading this book, the reader will have encountered nine different types of foundations—three public and six private. Exploring these different choices will make much more sense when the reader understands the important differences between public and private. So to begin, this book will (in part two) examine this important distinction and introduce three types of public charities (or public foundations). Next, six different types of private foundations will be defined (part three).

> **Note:** Those readers intending to form a private foundation may wish to read part three first. It may be helpful to have the private foundation options in mind before moving to part two.

In part four, the community foundation, a unique form of public charity, will be examined. With all these definitions and differences in mind, the book will next examine how to choose the right type of foundation to meet the reader's needs (part five). Finally, once the choice has been made as to which type of foundation best fits the reader's purpose, *First Steps* outlines the first legal steps necessary to establish the foundation (part six). When finished, the reader should be well prepared to begin these steps with legal counsel.

# PART TWO

Public v. Private

One of the most important distinctions in tax exempt law is the difference between public and private organizations. Since 1917, charitable organizations have been tax exempt. However, only since 1969 has the tax code drawn a clear line of demarcation between public charities and private foundations.

Within the philanthropic community, the term private foundation normally suggests that the organization has three distinct features: (1) it has one source of funding, usually one person, one family or one corporation; (2) the organization does not engage in direct charitable activities but instead makes grants to other charities to perform the service or activity; and (3) the funds available for the grants and the necessary administrative expenses come from endowment income.

As noted earlier, however, public charities and private foundations may both use the term foundation in their title. Depending on their technical tax classification, the rules that apply to each will be dramatically different. In this part, those differences will be examined closely, beginning with some brief historical background.

Prior to 1969, it was possible for a private individual (or family) to create a foundation, obtain a charitable tax deduction for making gifts to it and then control it in a private way with little public accountability. Beyond the requirement that the foundation had to be organized and operated exclusively for charitable purposes and had to file an annual tax return, the restrictions and rules were not very strict. Not surprisingly, a few people began to take advantage of this opportunity.[1] Following several Congressional investigations, the Treasury Department in 1965 published a report that documented certain problem areas. In response, Congress passed the 1969 Tax Reform Act, which, for the first time, defined a private foundation, clearly distinguishing it from public charities (or public foundations). Those organizations defined as private would henceforth be subject to a more comprehensive regulatory scheme.

---

[1] As an example, a donor could have created a foundation, given his closely held company to it, obtained a large tax deduction, continued to operate his business through the foundation, declared no dividends and made no grants to charitable organizations.

Definition of a Private Foundation

A central feature of the 1969 legislation was the enactment of Section 509 of the Internal Revenue Code. This section defines private foundations, and quite specifically draws the line between what is public and what is private. To understand this distinction, it is necessary to jump ahead for just a moment.

As will be explained in more detail in part six, no matter what type of foundation you are forming, you must first obtain legal recognition as a tax exempt charitable organization. In short, you must apply for, and obtain, a letter from the Internal Revenue Service that officially recognizes the foundation as exempt from income tax because it qualifies as a Section 501(c)(3) organization. Section 501 of the Internal Revenue Code defines many different organizations as exempt from federal income tax. Section 501(c)(3), however, is more specific. It defines as tax exempt all organizations that are "organized and operated exclusively for religious, charitable, scientific, testing for public safety, literary or educational purposes...." By obtaining classification as a Section 501(c)(3) organization, each new entity is not only exempt from income tax, but just as important, donations are tax deductible as charitable contributions. Why? Because, it is organized and operated exclusively for charitable purposes as required by the wording of Section 501(c)(3). In summary, whether the organization is a public charity or a private foundation is a secondary question; it must first be exempt from taxation and dedicated to charitable purposes under Section 501(c)(3).

Now back to Section 509. The tax code definition of a private foundation is somewhat strange. Instead of defining what a private foundation is, it defines what a private foundation is not. In short, Section 509 states that each Section 501(c)(3) organization is a private foundation unless it can demonstrate to the satisfaction of the IRS that it can qualify under at least one of four exceptions. On the next page, the reader will note a schematic illustration of Section 509. In reviewing this flow chart, you will see that the definition of a private foundation starts with all Section 501(c)(3) organizations (plus all governmental units) poured in at the top. But by the time all four exceptions have been funneled off, only private foundations remain. The first three exceptions (Traditional, Gross Receipts, and Supporting Organizations) are commonly referred to as public charities.

The consequences of being classified as a private foundation (falling to the bottom of the flow chart) as opposed to qualifying as one of the exceptions will be explained later, but first it is helpful to understand the underlying Congressional intent behind the decision to distinguish between public and private charitable organizations.

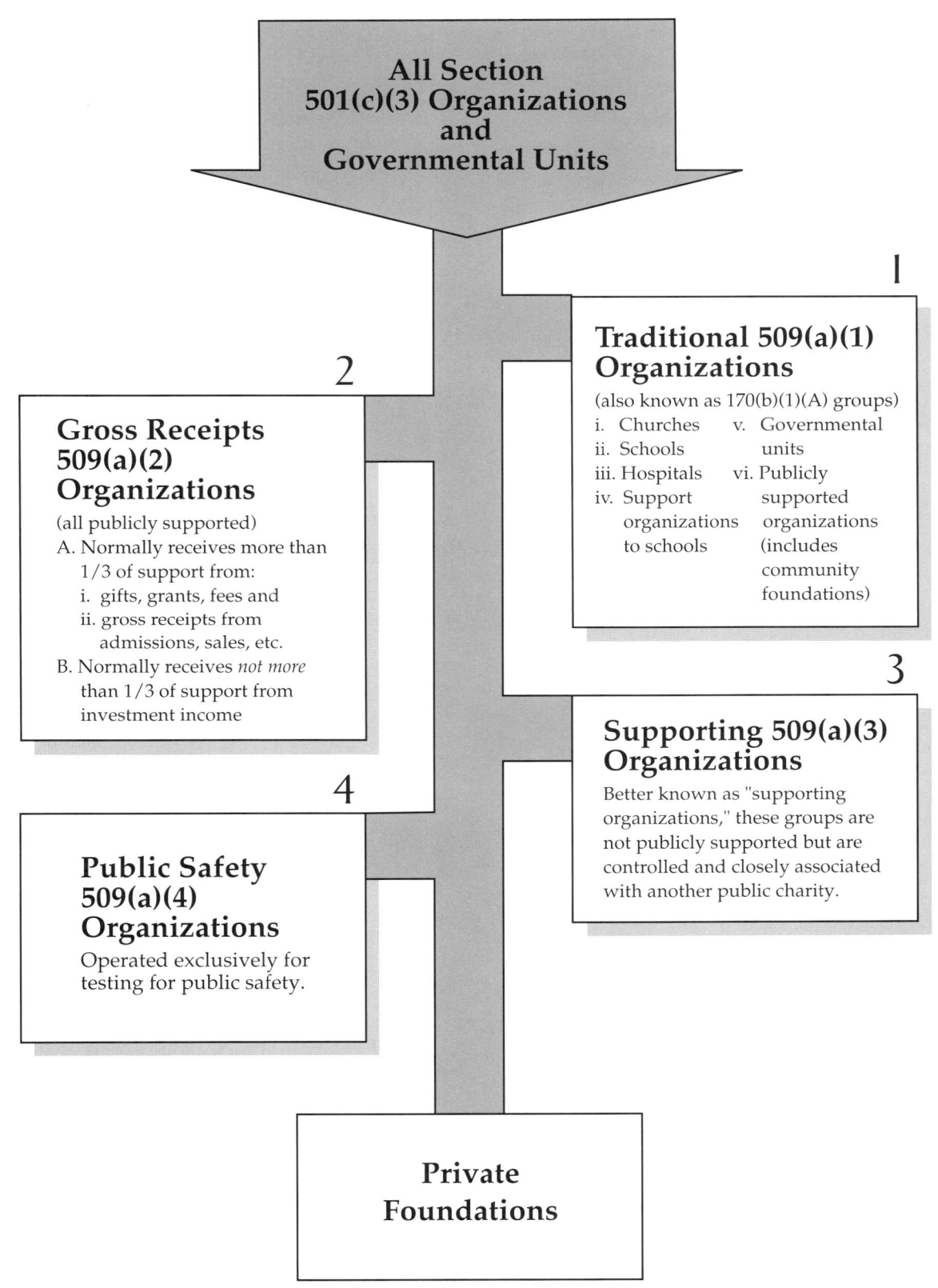

The Concept of Publicness

Faced with the issues raised by Congressional investigations and the 1965 Treasury Report, Congress determined that public charities should have some advantages over private foundations. This important decision was based in part on the assumption that where sufficient public involvement is present, fewer problems should arise.

In addition, Congress was interested in favoring the more timely effect of deductible contributions for charitable purposes. Public charities are more likely to apply their resources directly (and immediately) for charitable services; by comparison, private foundations are more apt to build up an endowment first which then regularly provides funding (out of investment income) to others to provide direct services.

The question then became: in the eyes of Congress what type of organization has a sufficient degree of publicness to avoid being classified as a private foundation? Four exceptions were written into the tax code, but only the first three represent public charities and, therefore, possible choices for the type of foundation that may be most suitable for the reader's purpose. Each of these three exceptions provides greater income tax benefits to the donor during lifetime and avoids the stricter rules applicable to private foundations.

Exception 1: Traditional Charities[2] and Publicly Supported Organization #1[3]

The traditional charity exception contains the largest number of organizations. The term traditional is not used in the tax code, but is offered here to distinguish the various categories in shorthand form.

This first exception is really a list of many different legal exceptions that include many traditional institutions: churches, colleges, universities, schools, nonprofit hospitals, medical research institutes, support organizations to schools and governmental units. If the organization qualifies under the legal definition of any one of these traditional institutions, it is sufficiently public and will not be classified as a private foundation.

Congress felt that churches were sufficiently public because by definition they were composed of a broad segment of the community that actively participated in the daily operations of the organization and contributed funds to it regularly. Similarly, educational institutions by definition include faculty, student bodies and parents paying tuition. Medical institutions (such as nonprofit hospitals) also could fall under the definition of public based on the involvement of the medical profession, and the fact that patients constantly use the institution for medical care. In short, each institution could not survive without continually convincing a reasonably large segment of the public that its operation and services are

---

[2] Technically referred to as Section 509(a)(1) organizations.
[3] In more legal terms, Section 170(b)(1)(A)(vi).

worthwhile. By similar reasoning, governmental units were sufficiently public, because their continued existence depended upon the oversight and approval of publicly elected officials. Note that all governmental units escape private foundation status through Exception 1. Governmental units are treated as public charities even though they are not usually classified under Section 501(c)(3).

A newly formed organization also can fall under this first exception as a traditional charity in another way. Even though it may not satisfy the legal definition of the various institutions just noted, it may qualify by being publicly supported. The test of publicness here is different. It is not the inherent nature (or definition) of the church, school or hospital that is important here. The question is whether the organization can meet certain public support tests. Can the organization demonstrate that a certain portion of its total support comes directly or indirectly from public contributions?

If one is contemplating forming an organization whose primary source of funding will be public donations or government support, the traditional charity format is the preferred type of organization to form. The organization will not be classified as a private foundation because it meets one of two public support tests (through Exception 1—Traditional). Traditional charities such as the Red Cross, the YMCA, the United Way and the Audubon Society meet this definition. However, certain organizations whose purpose primarily is grant-making (such as community foundations) also can satisfy the rules for this classification.

For publicly supported charities under this first exception, there are two tests. If the charity fails to meet the first test, it may fall back to the second test. The first test is called the **mechanical test** because it relies on a mathematical formula. If over the most recent four-year period, public support equals or exceeds one-third of total eligible support, the charity has met the test and qualifies as a public charity.

Public support divided by total support equals the support fraction.

The rules for what counts as public support and what does not are complex; this is one of many areas where legal counsel is especially important.[4] Generally, the types of support that count as *public* support and are included in both the top and the bottom half of the support fraction are:

1. Contributions from individuals, foundations, trusts or corporations.

2. Support from governmental units.

3. Membership dues, if the basic purpose of such payment is to support the organization rather than to purchase admissions, merchandise, services or the use of facilities.

---

[4] See Edie, John A., *How to Calculate the Public Support Test*, Council on Foundations, Washington, D.C. (1989).

All public support counts as part of total support. The types of support that *cannot* count as public support but are included in *total* support make up the bottom half of the fraction are:

1. Gross investment income.

2. Contributions and dues from individuals, foundations, trusts or corporations that exceed two percent of total support for the applicable period.[5]

3. Net income from unrelated business.

In constructing the support fraction to see if the one-third test is met, the organization must exclude from both the top and bottom half income received from exercising the exempt function of the foundation (admission fees, fees for service, etc.). See description of Publicly Supported Organization #2 (p. 11).

If the organization fails to meet the mechanical test for public support, it has a second chance and may resort to the **facts and circumstances test**. Under this test, the organization may fall below the one-third test, but—as the name suggests—it may still qualify as publicly supported depending on all the facts and circumstances. To qualify under this test, the organization must demonstrate adequate evidence of three different elements:

1. The total amount of government and public support must equal or exceed an absolute minimum ten percent of total support for the applicable period.

2. It must be organized and operated to attract new and additional public and governmental support on a continuous basis; and

3. It must demonstrate by other facts and circumstances that it is entitled to be recognized as public rather than private. Two of several factors considered here are; to what degree the board of directors represents the general public (rather than merely the donors), and to what extent services or facilities of the organization are available to the general public.

In summary, the first exception (Traditional Charities and Publicly Supported Organization #1) is quite flexible and meeting the public support requirements are not onerous. Consequently, it is the most frequently used form of public charity.

---

[5] For example, if total eligible support is $100,000 and one person gave $50,000, only $2,000 (two percent of total support) may be counted from that person as public support. The full $50,000 is counted in total support.

Note: The community foundation is an attractive option to consider. Community foundations are classified under this first exception—Publicly Supported Organization #1. Because a community foundation does not have a separate legal classification under the Tax Code, it is not described here. Part four describes the community foundation option.

Exception 2: Gross Receipts Charities or Publicly Supported Organization #2

The second type of public charity exception also must meet a public support test. Part of the legacy of the 1969 tax legislation was recognizing that certain organizations that relied in large part on gross receipts from tax-exempt activities also should qualify for the more favored tax advantages of the traditional charities. As noted above, the traditional charity may not include as public support any receipts obtained from carrying out its exempt function. A Gross Receipts charity—as the name suggests—can count such support as public. Again, the term gross receipts is not actually used in this section of the tax code, but it is offered here to avoid using more technical language.[6]

To qualify as a Gross Receipts charity, two tests must be met. The first is a different **public support test**. To satisfy this test, the organization normally must receive more than one-third of its total support from any combination of (1) qualifying gifts, grants, contributions or membership fees, *and* (2) gross receipts from admissions, sales of merchandise, performance of services or furnishing of facilities in activities related to its exempt functions. Examples of public charities that commonly fall under this classification are symphonies, opera companies and a wide variety of organizations that provide charitable services for a fee.

As with traditional charities, the support fraction is calculated over the previous four-year period. However, you have *no* facts and circumstances test to fall back on. The one-third public support percentage is an absolute minimum.

The second test that must be met is the **investment income test**. Under this test, the organization must show the total of its investment income and net unrelated business income does not exceed one-third of its total support.

It bears repeating that what constitutes total support versus public support for both Traditional charities and Gross Receipts charities is highly technical and complex and, therefore, skilled counsel is essential. Two examples of this complexity for Publicly Supported Charity #2 are worth noting.

---

[6] In legal terminology, Gross Receipts charities are Section 509(a)(2) organizations (see chart on p. 7).

Limits on Substantial Contributors. In adding up public support to qualify as a Publicly Supported Charity #2, the contribution of any amount from a disqualified person (including substantial contributors) cannot count as public support (in the top half) but nonetheless counts as total support (in the bottom half). A substantial contributor to a Publicly Supported Charity #2 is one who contributes more than $5,000; and that amount must exceed two percent of the total support ever received by the organization by the close of that tax year. Contributions from substantial contributors can count as public support for a traditional charity (subject to the two-percent limit described above).

$5,000 or One Percent Limit on Gross Receipts. A Gross Receipts charity cannot count as *public* support gross receipts from any person or governmental unit that exceeds the greater of $5,000 or one percent of total support for that year. However, any gross receipts that exceed this limit must be counted as part of *total* support in meeting the one-third test. As noted above, gross receipts received by a traditional charity cannot count as public support.

If this discussion of public support leaves you hopelessly confused, do not feel alone. The U.S. Tax Court stated that these rules are "almost frighteningly complex and technical." It is not the intention of this book to make the reader an expert on these definitions. However, you should be left with the understanding that: (1) two different types of publicly supported organization classifications are available, each with different advantages and disadvantages, and (2) sound legal advice on which option best fits the reader's needs is indispensable.

Exception 3: Supporting Organization[7]

The supporting organization is a third type of public charity category.[8] Because of the complexity of the rules, an attempt to provide details on how to qualify as a supporting organization would be foolish in the context of this book. Instead, the intent here is to provide a rough understanding of what a supporting organization is and how it can be used.

Four important points should be stressed. First, this option is becoming a popular choice among those starting foundations. Second, its requirements are flexible, enabling it to be used in a variety of circumstances. Third, its great advantage is that it does not require meeting any public support test, and, *at the same time*, it enables the organization to obtain the advantages of being a public charity. Finally, establishing a supporting organization without expert legal counsel is virtually impossible.

---

[7] In legal terminology, supporting organizations are known as Section 509(a)(3) organizations.

[8] Korman, R. and Gaske, W., *Supporting Organizations to Community Foundations: A Little-Used Alternative to Private Foundations*, Exempt Org. Tax Rev., 1327 (December 1994).

How does a supporting organization acquire sufficient publicness to qualify as a public charity? A supporting organization is like a barnacle; it attaches itself to (or supports) another public charity (or charities), and—in effect—acquires the public charity status of the organization or organizations it supports. The biggest problem is to make sure the barnacle sticks. The supporting organization must be carefully constructed to meet the complex tests required by the law and regulations. The two essential tests are a **purpose test** and a **control test**. The purpose test requires the supporting organization to benefit or carry out a purpose of the supported organization, ordinarily a public charity. The control test requires that the supported organization control the supporting organization. However, the definition of control is fairly broad and can be satisfied easily in most cases. Perhaps two examples of typical supporting organizations will aid the reader's understanding.

> **Trust example:** Mr. and Mrs. X endow a trust with $1 million to provide scholarships to public high school students in a particular city. The sole trustee is the local community foundation. No public support or fundraising is planned. The scholarships are paid from the investment income. The trust can qualify as a public charity because it is a supporting organization of a community foundation (one example of a traditional charity).
>
> **Corporate example:** Mr. and Mrs. Y establish a nonprofit corporation with an endowment of $1 million to help a local church relieve poverty in a particular city. In the articles of incorporation, they name a local church as the supported organization and the church appoints three of five members to the foundation's board. Mr. and Mrs. Y are the other two board members. This foundation can qualify as a public charity since it is a supporting organization of another public charity.

Two other general limitations are worth mentioning:

> **Specified public charities.** Normally it is expected the charity or charities that will be supported will be specifically identified in the governing instruments by name. However, under some circumstances, specific identification can be avoided by identifying beneficiary organizations by class or purpose so long as other more technical tests are also met.
>
> **Limitation on control.** A supporting organization may not be controlled directly or indirectly by one or more disqualified persons (meaning substantial contributors to the foundation and their families). Control in this context means having 50 percent or more of the voting power of the organization or the right to exercise veto power over the activities of the foundation.

The fourth exception from private foundation status is limited to organizations operated exclusively for public safety. Because such organizations do not normally undertake grantmaking, they are beyond the scope of this book. (See chart on p. 7)

Public v. Private: Effect on the Living Donor

Now that the reader has some basic information about the requirements for having an organization recognized as a public charity, what does it mean? What is the difference between a public charity and a private foundation? The differences fall into two important categories: the effects on the donor and the effects on the operations of the organization.

One of the major objectives of establishing a foundation is to create an organization to which contributions can be made that qualify as charitable deductions on the donor's income tax return. It is a crucial fact that the amount the donor may deduct depends on whether the donee organization is classified as public or private. Three important differences exist and they favor public charities. Congress established these preferences for public charities on the theory that donations to them would be used more quickly to provide needed charitable services. Public charities are likely to be direct service agencies, whereas private foundations frequently use their funds to set up endowments first, and then make grants out of investment income. The three limitations explained here only affect gifts by *living* donors under the income tax. Gifts by bequest after the death of the donor are regulated by estate tax rules and contain no such limitations.

Percentage Limits on Gifts of Cash

In any given tax year, an individual donor may contribute cash to a tax exempt charitable organization and treat the gift as a charitable contribution that is deductible in calculating his or her income tax. If the donee organization is public, the donor may deduct an amount equal to as much as 50 percent of his or her income (adjusted gross income). However, if the organization is classified as private, the annual deduction of cash may not exceed 30 percent of income.[9]

Percentage Limits on Gifts of Appreciated Property

The limits on gifts of appreciated property are different. Appreciated property is long-term capital gain property such as stocks, bonds, land or tangible personal property (paintings, manuscripts, etc.).[10] Here, if the donee organization is considered public, the donor may deduct an amount equal to as much as 30 percent of adjusted gross income. If the donee is private, the limit is 20 percent of income.

---

[9] In part three, we will see how certain private foundations can qualify for the higher limits.
[10] Gifts of tangible personal property may not be fully deductible unless the property is actually used for the charitable purposes of the donee organization.

Five-Year Carryover

If in any year, the donor exceeds any of the limits noted above, he or she may carry over the excess of these limits for the next five tax years, regardless of whether the donee is considered public or private. Prior to the Deficit Reduction Act of 1984, there was no carryover of any kind for gifts to private foundations.

Limits on Value of Gifts of Appreciated Property

In addition to those percentage limitations on gifts of appreciated property (30 percent to public and 20 percent to private), the donor must keep another important difference in mind. Whether or not the donor can deduct the full, fair market value of the gift of appreciated property within those ceilings depends on whether the donor organization is treated as public or private. If the gift is made to a public foundation, the donor may deduct 100 percent of the fair market value of appreciated property (within the percentage limitations). However, if the gift is made to a private foundation, the donor may deduct only his or her cost (or basis) in the property. At this writing (October 1997), the Council on Foundations is working to have Congress make permanent a provision that permits the donor to deduct 100 percent of the fair market value *if* the gift to a private foundation is one of publicly traded stock (not closely held stock, not bonds, not land, not tangible personal property).[11]

Note, however that gifts of most kinds of appreciated property may be fully deductible if the private foundation receiving the gift qualifies as a conduit foundation (see p. 28) or an operating foundation (see p. 29).

---

[11] Section 170(e)(5) was added to the tax code in 1984 but expired after 10 years on December 31, 1994. It was restored for 11 months from July 1, 1996 through May 31, 1997, and extended once again from June 1, 1997 through June 30, 1998.

PUBLIC v. PRIVATE: EFFECTS ON LIVING DONOR

	PUBLIC CHARITY and COMMUNITY FOUNDATIONS	PRIVATE FOUNDATION
Gifts of Cash	50% Limit	30% Limit
Gifts of Appreciated Property	30% Limit (a)	20% Limit
Carryover	5 Years	5 Years
Value of Appreciated Property That Can Be Deducted (b)	100% of Fair Market Value for all Types	Cost Only for all types of Appreciated Property Except for Publicly Traded Stock (c)

Note: The above limitations apply *only* to income tax deductions. They do *not* apply to estate taxes. Gifts at death (bequests) to public or private foundations are not subject to any of these limitations.

  a) When making gifts of appreciated property, the donor may take advantage of the higher 50 percent limit if he or she is willing to deduct only cost.

  b) Gifts of tangible personal property (such as art work) must be deducted at cost if the use of the property by the donee is unrelated to its exempt purpose.

  c) Gifts of nonpublicly traded stock and other types of appreciated property are generally deductible only at cost. The ability to deduct the full market value of publicly traded stock under Section 170 (e)(5) of the Tax Code expired on December 31, 1994; the Council on Foundations successfully persuaded Congress in 1995 to restore this valuable provision from July 1, 1996 until May 31, 1997. Legislation in 1997 extended the provision 13 additional months until June 30, 1998. Donors should consult with their tax advisors for current availability of this code section.

Example: A donor with adjusted gross income of $100,000 wants to give $60,000 in cash to the local museum that is a public charity. For that year, the 50 percent limitation on gifts of cash will limit her deduction to $50,000 (50 percent of $100,000). The remaining $10,000 can be carried over to the next year. If the same donor had, instead, given $60,000 to her family foundation, only $30,000 would be deductible because of the 30 percent limitation for gifts of cash to private foundations. The remaining $30,000 could be carried over and deducted in the next year.

Example: Assume the same facts as stated above, concerning the $60,000 gift to the family foundation. What are the tax savings to the donor? By giving $60,000 in cash to her family foundation, the donor reduces her taxable income from $100,000 to $70,000 for that year. The tax savings will depend on her marginal tax bracket. If her tax bracket is 31 percent, she will reduce her tax payment to IRS by $9,300 (31 percent times $30,000 in reduced taxable income). She can carry over the remaining $30,000 to the next year and assuming her taxable income before the gift is again $100,000, she will save $9,300 in taxes in the next year.

Public v. Private: Effect on the Organization

In passing the Tax Reform Act of 1969, Congress was determined to halt certain practices of a few charitable organizations that were controlled privately. As a result, a central part of this watershed legislation was a comprehensive system defining and regulating private foundations. In effect, Congress was saying it would permit the continued existence of private foundations but only with some clearly defined limitations. *Public charities are not subject to most of these rules.* (See comparison chart on p. 49).

Prior to 1969, the main enforcement tool available to the Internal Revenue Service was the authority to revoke the tax exempt status of a public charity or private foundation. No matter how large or small the infraction, terminating the organization was the only sanction. For example, where the infractions merely were occasional or minor and IRS had difficulty making a revocation of tax status stand up in court. In addition, the penalty did not directly affect the person responsible, but put the organization out of business. In response to Treasury recommendations, Congress installed a system of alternative penalty taxes that could be levied against the private foundation and, in certain cases, against the private foundation manager. This regulatory system of penalty taxes has worked so well that Congress, in more limited fashion, has established similar rules for certain activities by public charities. Here is a summary of the regulatory system established by Congress in 1969 to limit certain activities of private foundations.[12] It is followed by a description of more recent laws that penalize public charities.

Two Percent Excise Tax on Investment Income (Section 4940)

To pay for the additional cost of auditing and monitoring private foundations, the law requires each private foundation to pay an annual excise tax equal to two percent of net investment income. Originally, the tax was four percent but it was cut in half in 1978 because it was generating income far in excess of what was necessary to cover the added regulatory costs of the IRS. Since 1985, a private foundation could reduce its excise tax to one percent, providing its qualifying distributions for the year meet certain requirements.

Tax on Acts of Self-Dealing (Section 4941)

A private foundation generally is prohibited from entering into any financial transaction with certain related persons defined in the law as disqualified persons. This prohibition applies whether or not the transaction is fair and reasonable, or benefits the private foundation. Disqualified persons include trustees, directors, foundation managers with similar powers, substantial contributors to the foundation, and certain family members of the above (including spouses and children). The prohibited transactions include: (1) selling, exchanging,

---

[12] For a more extensive discussion, see Edie, John A., *Family Foundations and the Law: What You Need to Know*, Council on Foundations, Washington, D.C. (1995).

or leasing property, (2) lending money or extending credit, and (3) furnishing goods, services or facilities. The paying of compensation to a trustee, director, officer or foundation manager for personal services is a permissible exception, as long as the compensation is necessary and reasonable. Where violations occur, an initial penalty tax of five percent of the amount involved is levied on the self-dealer. Similar, but less comprehensive legislation is in effect, limiting certain financial transactions of public charities; namely excessive compensation and non-fair market value transactions with disqualified persons. These limitations generally are referred to as intermediate sanctions (see below).

Tax on Failure to Meet Minimum Distribution (Section 4942)

Every private foundation is required to pay annually an amount equal to five percent of its net investment assets in the form of qualifying distributions. There is no reduced distribution requirement for new private foundations. For example, in general terms, a private foundation with investment assets of $1 million is required to make qualifying distributions equal to roughly $50,000 for that year (five percent times $1 million). Failure to meet this payout requirement will result in an initial penalty tax of 15 percent of the shortfall. The foundation has 12 months after the end of the tax year to make up any shortfall in the payout.

Qualifying distributions include grants to qualified charities as well as all necessary and reasonable administrative costs to make those grants. Qualifying distributions also may include costs to provide direct charitable activities (such as conducting in-house medical research and publishing the results) and costs to acquire assets used directly in conducting the foundation's exempt activities (such as purchasing computer equipment to track the foundation's grant or financial activities).

Tax on Excess Business Holdings (Section 4943)

In general, private foundations specifically are prohibited from controlling any business. Although the rules are complex, for most purposes a private foundation may not hold more than 20 percent ownership in any business. The limit may be 35 percent if effective control of the corporation is in the hands of one or more persons who are third parties not disqualified. In staying below this limit, the private foundation must count or add in the shares held by all disqualified persons. However, if the foundation itself owns less than two percent of the company, it does not matter what percentage is held by disqualified persons.

If a private foundation is endowed with shares which, when added to shares held by the donor and other disqualified persons, exceed 20 percent ownership in a company, the foundation is required to divest itself of enough shares to drop below the limit within five years. Public charities are not subject to this limitation. Failure to divest within the time required will subject the foundation to an initial tax of five percent of the amount held in excess of the limit.

Tax on Jeopardy Investments (Section 4944)

This code section prohibits any investment by a private foundation that might jeopardize its exempt purpose. Generally speaking, an investment is considered a violation of this rule if it is determined that the board of directors or trustees, in making such an investment, failed to exercise ordinary business care and prudence under the facts and circumstance prevailing at the time of the investment. An initial tax of five percent of the amount of the investment is levied on the foundation for any such violation, and a tax of five percent may be levied on the foundation manager. No category of investment is a violation per se, but certain types of investment will be closely scrutinized by the IRS (trading in commodities futures, selling short, etc.) Risky investments, however, may be permitted if they qualify as program-related investments where their primary purpose is to achieve a charitable objective rather than produce income.[13]

Tax on Taxable Expenditures (Section 4945)

In addition to the regulation of foundation operations listed above, Congress also set out a list of restrictions on certain types of grant activity. Generally, an initial tax of ten percent of the amount involved can be levied on a private foundation (and 2.5 percent on the foundation manager) for any of the following expenditures:

1. **Lobbying.** Any expenditure to carry on propaganda, or otherwise attempt to influence legislation.[14]

2. **Electioneering and Voter Registration.** Any expenditure to influence the outcome of any specific public election,[15] or to carry on, directly or indirectly, a voter registration drive.

3. **Grants to Individuals.** Any grant to an individual for travel, study or similar purposes.

4. **Grants to Non-Charities.** A grant to any organization that is not a recognized public charity (Traditional charity, Gross Receipts charity or Supporting Organization; see discussion on pp. 7-13)

---

[13] *Program-Related Investment Primer*, Council on Foundations, 120 pp. (1993).
[14] Public charities may also be subject to penalty for excessive lobbying under IRC Section 4912.
[15] Effective December 22, 1987, any political campaign expenditures by public charities also are subject to penalty tax.

5. **Expenditures for Non-Charitable Purposes.**

Each of the first four prohibited activities listed above have exceptions, and those running a private foundation would be well advised to consult legal counsel before attempting such a program. Listed below are some of the exceptions the law permits:

- Expenditures for lobbying are permitted in certain limited circumstances including: (1) in self-defense to influence legislation that would affect the tax-exempt status of, or the deductibility of gifts to, private foundations; or (2) in response to a written request from a legislative body.[16]

- Grants for voter registration are permitted if several conditions are met. Two of the conditions are: (1) the grantee's activities must be nonpartisan and not confined to one election; and (2) the grantee must carry on its activities in five or more states.

- Grants to individuals for study or travel (scholarships, fellowships, prizes or awards) are permitted if certain specific requirements are met, including: (1) the grant is awarded on an objective and nondiscriminatory basis; and (2) the grant is made pursuant to a procedure approved *in advance* by the IRS.[17]

- Grants to organizations that are not public charities (Traditional charities, Gross Receipts charities or Supporting Organizations) are permitted if they are for charitable purposes and the private foundation is willing to exercise expenditure responsibility, a legal requirement wherein the grantor must make certain that the grant is used solely for charitable purposes. In summary, expenditure responsibility requires: (1) a pre-grant inquiry of the grantee, (2) a written agreement specifying the charitable purposes for which the funds must be used, and requiring the grantee to comply with certain legal requirements, (3) regular written status reports from the grantee, and 4) inclusion of a description of the grant and its status on the private foundation's tax return.

- Grants to organizations outside the United States are possible by both private foundations and public charities. Such grants generally require different types of documentation to show that the grantee is the equivalent of a U.S. charity, or (if not such an equivalent) that some form of expenditure responsibility has been followed by the granting foundation.

---

[16] See Edie, John A., *Foundations and Lobbying: Safe Ways to Affect Public Policy*, Council on Foundations, Washington, D.C. (1991).

[17] See Beckwith, Edward J., Baker & Hostetler, *Grants to Individuals by Private Foundations*, Council on Foundations, Washington, D.C. (1995).

Regulatory Scheme for Public Charities—1996 Intermediate Sanctions

In 1996, Congress added penalties to public charities designed to follow the penalty tax approach used for private foundations in 1969. However, these new sanctions are more limited.[18] Better known as intermediate sanctions, these provisions are relatively new and no regulations have been issued yet (as of September 1997) so that IRS has not been enforcing them to any great degree.

The new law is applicable to all Section 501(c)(3) and 501(c)(4) organizations (but not private foundations) and is RETROACTIVE for any excess benefit transactions made after September 14, 1995. The Act gives the IRS authority to impose excise tax penalties on disqualified persons (insiders) who receive excess benefits either through compensation or some form of financial transaction (sale, lease, etc.). Similar penalties can be applied to organization managers who participate in approving such transactions with the knowledge that they will provide excess benefits. No penalty tax can be applied to the organization itself, although egregious cases may still result in removal of tax-exempt status.

Disqualified persons are defined as individuals who are in a position to exercise substantial influence over the affairs of the organization, whether by virtue of being an organization's manager (officer, director, etc.) or otherwise. An excess benefit transaction occurs when a disqualified person: (a) engages in a non-fair market value transaction with the organization (the organization does not get fair value); (b) receives unreasonable compensation from the organization; or (c) receives payment based on a revenue-sharing arrangement that is not permitted. Generally, for compensation purposes, reasonable means how are like persons compensated for like responsibilities and work in similar organizations. The IRS will apply existing tax law standards for fair market value determinations.

The tax is two-tiered. The first level of penalty is 25 percent of the excess benefit on the disqualified person and 10 percent on an organization manager ($10,000 maximum) who participates in the transaction knowing it to be excessive. The second tier is 200 percent of the excess benefit on the disqualified person if the transaction is not corrected in a specified time period.

---

[18] Taxpayer Bill of Rights 2 (H.R. 2337), Pub. L. No. 104-168, 110 Stat. 1452, signed by the President on July 30, 1996.

Reporting Requirements (Section 6033)

Except for religious organizations, every 501(c)(3) organization (public or private) must file an annual information return with the IRS. Public charities with annual gross receipts less than $25,000 are exempt from this requirement. Public charities file the Form 990 and private foundations file the Form 990-PF. Both of these forms require much of the same information, including:

1. Gross income for the year;

2. Expenses attributable to producing such income;

3. A balance sheet showing assets, liabilities and net worth as of the beginning and the end of the year;

4. Disbursements within the year for exempt purposes;

5. Total contributions and gifts received, and the names and addresses of all substantial contributors; and

6. Names, addresses and compensation of officers, directors and highly compensated employees.

Both the Form 990 and the Form 990-PF are public documents and may be obtained from the IRS. However, the names and addresses of substantial contributors to public charities are not public information and, thus, are not made available by IRS.

In addition, there are a few additional types of information that must be provided to IRS by *private* foundations. These additional reporting requirements include:

1. An itemized statement of securities and all other assets at the close of the year;

2. An itemized statement of all grants made or approved for future payment including the name and address of each grantee, and the purpose and amount of each grant; and

3. The address of the principal office of the foundation and (if different) the place where its books and records are kept.

Finally, each *private* foundation must make its return available for public inspection at the principal office of the foundation during regular business hours for requests made within 180 days after the date of publication of its availability. Such publication must be made no later that the day required for filing the return with the IRS and notice of the availability of the return must be published along with the foundation's telephone number in a newspaper having general circulation in the county of the principal office.

Beginning with the 1987 Form 990, a public charity is required to make its return available for public inspection for three years after the date of filing. Legislation in 1996 increased this requirement for public charities by requiring that they provide certain documents as take home copies. Public charities must provide to any individual a copy of the Form 990 (up to three years back) or the Form 1023 (application for exempt status) "without charge other than a reasonable fee for any reproduction and mailing costs." Persons requesting in person must be provided copies immediately; those requesting in writing must be provided within 30 days. Violations are now subject to a fine of $5,000 for each failure to provide a return or application. The Secretary of the Treasury has authority to issue regulations waiving these requirements where the organization has made such documents "widely available" or where there is evidence of a harassment campaign.[19]

Regardless of legal requirements, the Council on Foundations encourages all foundations (whether public charity or private foundation) to make take home copies available for those who request them. The Council also encourages foundations to make regular reports on their grantmaking activities to the Foundation Center and to local regional associations of grantmakers.

Summary of Part Two

You have now reviewed the basic difference between public charities and private foundations. Three types of public charity have been described: Traditional, Gross Receipts and Supporting Organization including the tests each must satisfy to become a public charity rather than a private foundation.

Clearly, there are several reasons for preferring to be public. Why, then, form a private foundation? The answer to that question is in part three.

---

[19] Taxpayer Bill of Rights 2 (H.R. 2337), Pub. L. No. 104-168, 110 Stat. 1452, signed by the President on July 30, 1996. The actual effective date for the "take home" copy requirement is 60 days after the Treasury Department issues regulations (expected to be late 1998). See code section 6104.

PART THREE

What is a Private Foundation?

Deciding what type of foundation to form is not limited to questions of legal restriction or regulation. In fact, for many who choose the private foundation option the goal is to maximize independence to be innovative and responsive. The directors of private foundations (unlike elected officials) are not subject to constant review by voters. Similarly, unlike corporations, they are not responsible to shareholders. And, unlike many public charities, they need not conduct regular fundraising drives. This unique flexibility of private foundations was perhaps best summarized by a Treasury Department report in 1965:

"Private philanthropy plays a special and vital role in our society. Beyond providing for areas which government cannot or should not advance (such as religion), private philanthropic organizations can be uniquely qualified to initiate thought and action, experiment with new and untried ventures, dissent from prevailing attitudes and act quickly and flexibly.

"Private foundations have an important part in this work. Available even to those of relatively restricted means, they enable individuals or small groups to establish new charitable endeavors and to express their own bents, concerns and experience. In doing so, they enrich the pluralism of our social order. Equally important, because their funds are frequently free of commitment to specific operating programs, they can shift the focus of their interest and their financial support from one charitable area to another. They can, hence, constitute a powerful instrument for evolution, growth and improvement in the shape and direction of charity."

Private foundations usually have one source of funding. The endowment or the regular contributions that provide the foundation's resources come from a single source; one person, one family, one company or a small group of donors. This good fortune creates another advantage. Because the donor or donors have sufficient wealth to establish and continue the activities of the foundation, they may avoid the often cumbersome and costly requirement of meeting a public support test, which may entail either hiring professional fundraisers or regularly organizing special fundraising events.

But what about the regulations governing the conduct of private foundations? To many donors, these restrictions do not pose serious problems. While they may not be overjoyed with paying a two percent (or one percent) excise tax on investment income, it is not onerous. Moreover, they have no intention of conducting any activities that have been limited or proscribed by Congress. Specifically: (1) they have no intention of entering into any self-dealing transactions with disqualified persons; (2) they see no problem in meeting the minimum five percent payout requirement; (3) they intend to diversify their investments and do not want to own a large share of any business; (4) they certainly would not consider jeopardizing the assets of the foundation through any risky investments; and (5) they are not interested in certain areas of grantmaking that could cause problems (lobbying, voter registration, grants to individuals, etc.) or they are willing to abide by the additional restrictions. In addition, the more detailed tax return required for private foundations does not seem much more complicated than what is required for public charities.

When analyzed, the many restrictions on private foundations are not necessarily that difficult. Existing private foundations have learned to live with these rules comfortably. For a closer examination of why a donor would choose either a private foundation or a public charity, see part five.

As you learned in part two, the tax consequences to the living donor for giving to a private foundation are sometimes not as favorable as those for giving to a public charity. As a result, the tax effects of a particular gift must be carefully reviewed by the donor. But there are other ways in which a donor may give to a private foundation and still take advantage of the most liberal rules affecting the deductibility of the charitable gift. (See later discussions of conduits, pooled common funds and operating foundations beginning on p. 28)

General Use of the Term Foundation

As mentioned in the introduction, the term foundation is used loosely to apply to organizations of differing characteristics. When an organization uses the word foundation in its title, it reveals little. The word does not explain whether or not the organization is public or private, for example; and as pointed out in part two, that distinction is of vital importance.

However, to those active in the field of philanthropy, the term foundation (when used alone) takes on a definite meaning. In its more common usage, it suggests an organization whose primary purpose is to make grants to other charitable entities; and usually means the organization's main or only source of income is its endowment. All grants and administrative expenses are paid solely from investment income. A foundation normally is *not* a fundraising or grantseeking organization, and in most cases it is private rather than public. This general rule has exceptions. For example, private *operating* foundations usually do not make grants. Also, community foundations normally have endowments and make grants, yet they are not private foundations and regularly seek public support (see part four). In each of these cases, however, the term foundation is normally not used alone—usually such organizations are mentioned specifically as *operating* foundations or *community* foundations.

In part two, the three tax classifications known as public charities—Traditional, Gross Receipts and Supporting Organizations—were introduced. The six types of private foundations will now be defined.

Independent Foundation

Occasionally in the form of a trust, but usually organized as a nonprofit corporation, the independent foundation is the most common type of private foundation. Sometimes it is referred to as a family foundation when the donor or the donor's relatives are still involved. Because it usually does not operate directly any charitable service or activity, it is sometimes called a private non-operating foundation. In 1997, more than 40,000 independent foundations operated nationwide with assets ranging in size from under $10,000 to more than $10 billion. Most, but not all, have endowments and their funds usually are obtained from a single source: individual, family or corporation. They are managed by their own trustees or board of directors. Although the independent foundation may operate its own charitable activity or service directly (in house), the bulk of its budget each year usually is made up of grants to other charitable organizations which in turn provide the services or activity to the public.[20]

Company Foundation

In virtually every respect, the company foundation, or the corporate foundation, is a private foundation subject to the same rules applicable to an independent foundation. In this case, however, the source of funds is a for-profit company. Technically, the corporate foundation is a separate legal entity (usually a nonprofit corporation). Despite the separate legal status, the corporate foundation normally is closely tied to the corporation that provides the funding.

While most company foundations have an endowment, it usually is small—perhaps two or three times the annual grant budget. For the most part, grants made by a company foundation are derived from charitable contributions received from the parent company in the same year. The funds simply pass through (although the foundation is rarely a conduit foundation; see p. 28). By building up a small endowment in the foundation, the company can maintain a reserve for low profit years and thus keep the level of its contributions budget steady even though the profit/loss picture is fluctuating.

The board of directors of a company foundation usually is made up of corporate officials who make decisions on grant recipients. Occasionally, the board will include individuals with no affiliation with the sponsoring corporation. Sometimes grant decisions are made by local company officials in different parts of the country who follow agreed-upon procedures and submit their decisions to the foundation for action. Grantmaking by company foundations

---

[20] The best source of research information on private foundations is the Foundation Center, which maintains a nationwide network of reference collections for free public use. Each state has at least one cooperating collection. At a minimum, the reader should be aware of the Center's main publication—*The Foundation Directory*—which lists the largest foundations in America. The Center also publishes each year *Foundation Giving*, which provides a wealth of tables, charts and factual analysis of the foundation field. A list of the Center's publications is included in the list of references.

tends to be in fields related to corporate activities or in communities where the corporation operates. It is also common for companies to maintain a separate corporate contributions budget that makes grants directly to charities in addition to the grants made through the foundation. Because of certain rules restricting private foundations, some types of contributions are better made from the corporation: loaned executives, benefit tickets or gifts of inventory.[21]

Conduit or Pass-Through Foundation

The conduit foundation is a private non-operating foundation subject to all the rules and regulations noted above and frequently is used by a donor during his or her lifetime to establish the foundation and develop its policies so it is ready to accept a much larger infusion of funds at the death of the donor. Although it is a private foundation, donors to it may take advantage of all the more liberal limitations on charitable deductions applicable to gifts made to public charities (see p. 16 for comparison). This special exception has a price tag: all the contributions must flow through or pass through the conduit foundation within two and one-half months after the end of the tax year in which the gifts are made. More specifically, for the tax-year in question the conduit foundation must meet its normal payout requirements and make qualifying distributions (grants to charitable organizations plus eligible administrative costs) equal to 100 percent of the value of its contributions received during the tax year by the 15th day of the third month following the close of the tax year. A private foundation may elect to be or not to be a conduit foundation from year to year.

For obvious reasons, conduit foundations are used by living donors and are not the classification of choice for bequests. Consistently throughout the tax code, Congress permits living donors to take advantage of the most liberal contribution limits where the gifts will be applied directly to charitable services. Here the gifts must pass through during a 14-1/2 month period (maximum) to grantee charitable organizations and may not be used to augment the foundation endowment.

Pooled Common Funds

One rarely used form of private foundation is beginning to attract more interest particularly by community foundations (described in part four). Usually referred to as the pooled common fund or donor directed depository, it resembles the supporting organization (the Section 509(a)(3) public charity described in part two) except that the donor retains much more control over the eventual disposition of the funds. Because of this control, and the

---

[21] See Coy, John F., *When Corporate Foundations Make Sense*, Council on Foundations (Washington, D.C., 1994), 24 pp.; Edie, John A., *Corporate Giving and The Law: Steering Clear of Trouble*, Council on Foundations (Washington, D.C., 1992), 24 pp.; and Beckwith, Edward J., et. al., *Company Foundations and The Self Dealing Rules*, Council on Foundations (Washington, D.C., 1993), 30 pp.

resulting lack of publicness, the organization is classified as a private foundation and is subject to the stricter regulatory rules described earlier.

However, despite its private foundation status, the donor may use all the most favorable rules for any charitable deductions made to it. A price is paid for this advantage, however, as explained by the following rules, which describe a pooled common fund private foundation:

1. One or many donors may make contributions which are then pooled into a common fund.

2. The donor (or his or her spouse) may *retain the right* to designate annually the organizations to which the income attributable to his or her contributions shall be given.

3. The donee organizations must be only traditional charities—as described under Section 509(a)(1).

4. The fund must be required by its governing instrument to distribute, and it *must in fact* pay out (including administrative costs):

    a. All its adjusted net income to one or more eligible charities not later than the 15th day of the third month after the close of the taxable year in which such income was earned or realized; and

    b. All the corpus attributable to any donor's contribution to the fund to one or more eligible charities not later than one year after the death of the donor (or the donor's surviving spouse if such spouse has the right to designate the recipients of such corpus).

Operating Foundation

An operating foundation is a private foundation subject to nearly all the applicable restrictions and reporting requirements noted above. In addition, it must directly carry out its own charitable purposes. However, donors to a private operating foundation may take advantage of the more liberal charitable deduction rules applicable to gifts to public charities (see p. 16 for comparison). In this way, operating foundations are similar to conduit foundations (see p. 28). Here, too, a price is paid for this special advantage to the living donor: to qualify as an operating foundation, the foundation must spend substantially all (85 percent) of its net investment income directly for the active conduct of its own exempt activities (as opposed to making grants).

Although some operating foundations make a limited number of grants, they commonly operate museums, libraries, nursing homes, orphanages, research institutes or historic preservation parks. Most often, operating foundations obtain their operating funds from an endowment created by the original donor; it is also possible for an operating foundation to have no endowment and receive its operating funds through annual contributions from one donor or a small number of donors. However, because the number of donors is so small the foundation is not able to meet one of the public support tests which would permit it to avoid private foundation status altogether.

The specific rules for qualification as an operating foundation are complicated and no attempt will be made here to cover them in complete detail. In forming an operating foundation, skilled legal counsel is necessary. Here is a summary of the requirements.

Every operating foundation must satisfy the **income test**. In simple terms the income test requires the operating foundation to use substantially all of its income directly for the active conduct of its charitable activities—not for grants to other organizations. To pass the income test, the operating foundation must spend on its own operations the smaller of these two amounts:

1. 85 percent of its adjusted net income from investments, or

2. 4.25 percent of its net investment assets.

Expenses for the production of income (fees to investment managers, for example) cannot be counted in meeting the income test. An operating foundation may count only administrative and operating expenses necessary to carry out its charitable programs.

Under limited circumstances, grants or scholarships to individuals may count in meeting the income test. To qualify, such grants must be made to individuals to accomplish an exempt purpose that is directly related to the conduct of the programs in which the operating foundation has a 'significant involvement." For example, grants by the foundation to individuals to engage in scientific research projects under the direction and supervision of the foundation would qualify.

In addition to the income test, each operating foundation must satisfy one of these three tests:

The Assets Test. To meet the assets test, an operating foundation must show that at least 65 percent of all its assets are devoted directly to the active conduct of the charitable activities. Assets held for the production of income (stocks, bonds and other endowment funds) are part of the total assets but do not count in satisfying the 65 percent rule. Examples of qualifying assets are physical facilities (museums, nursing homes) and the land they occupy; classroom fixtures, equipment and research facilities; and intangible assets such as patents, copyrights and trademarks to the extent they are used in carrying out the foundation's exempt activities.

The Endowment Test. To meet the endowment test, the operating foundation normally must expend funds directly for the active conduct of its charitable purposes equal to three and one-third percent of the fair market value of its net investment assets. By comparison, private non-operating foundation must meet a minimum payout of five percent of net investment assets. Operating foundations can avoid this three and one-third percent minimum payout, of course, by satisfying a test other than the endowment test. In many cases where the endowment is small, satisfaction of the income test will also satisfy this test.

The Support Test. To satisfy the support test, an operating foundation must meet the following three requirements:

1. 85 percent of its support normally must be received from the general public and from five or more unrelated exempt organizations. Gross investment income does not count as public support. Support from one exempt organization will count as public support only if there is support from four other exempt organizations. Treasury regulations permit an organization to satisfy this requirement with support from five exempt organizations and not support from the general public.

2. Not more than 25 percent of its support normally may be received from any one exempt organization.

3. Not more than 50 percent of its total support may be from gross investment income.

In applying these tests, the operating foundation is permitted to aggregate relevant financial data covering a four-year period. This period includes the current tax year and the preceding three tax years. In the alternative, an operating foundation may show that it satisfied the income test and one of the additional three test in three of four years (current year plus three preceding years).

A newly created foundation seeking classification as an operating foundation may file an application with the IRS showing that it can reasonably be expected to meet the income test and one of the other three tests in its first year. It must then meet the applicable tests by the end of its first year to continue its classification as an operating foundation for its second year.

Exempt Operating Foundation

The 1984 Tax Reform Act introduced a hybrid classification of private foundation. This category of private foundation can provide substantial advantages to operating foundations that were in existence on January 1, 1983, and for some publicly supported charities with at least ten years of operation. This sixth type of private foundation is *not* a viable option for anyone planning to create a new charitable organization. Congress specifically designated this new classification to resolve problems of existing organizations, not to create an option for new entities.

The characteristics of an exempt operating foundation are identical to those of a regular operating foundation with two exceptions: (1) the exempt operating foundation is not required to pay an excise tax on net investment income, and (2) other private foundations may make grants to it without the necessity of exercising expenditure responsibility. Normally, private foundations may not make grants to other private foundations (including private operating foundations) without incurring the added administrative workload of expenditure responsibility, which requires the grantor private foundation to: (1) make a pre-grant inquiry; (2) enter into a specific written agreement with the grantee; (3) obtain periodic and regular status reports from the grantee; and (4) indicate on its tax return the status of the grant. Failure to exercise expenditure responsibility (or failure to do it correctly) will subject the private foundation grantor to a penalty tax. Many private non-operating foundations as a matter of policy will not make grants requiring expenditure responsibility. In short, a regular operating foundation will be a much more attractive grantee if it can obtain this exempt status.

Similarly, existing publicly supported charities (at least 10-years old) who are on the verge of being reclassified as private foundations because their investment income is greatly outpacing their public support can also become exempt operating foundations. In fact, it was just for these public charities that the new classification was formed.

To qualify as an exempt operating foundation, three tests must be met:

1. **Organizational Status Test.** The organization must either:

    a. Have been classified as an operating foundation on January 1, 1983; or

    b. Be classified as a public charity and have met the applicable public support test for at least ten taxable years.

2. **Public Board Test.** The governing body of the organization must meet two requirements:

   a. It must consist of individuals at least 75 percent of whom are not disqualified individuals. Disqualified individuals are: (1) substantial contributors, (2) owners of 20 percent or more of a business or partnership that is a substantial contributor, and (3) members of the families of such owners or contributors.

   b. The board must be broadly representative of the general public.

3. **Disqualified Individual Test.** At no time during the taxable year can the organization have an officer who is a disqualified individual as defined in 2(a) above.

The basic characteristics for three types of public foundations and six types of private foundation have now been outlined. Before examining why a donor might choose one form over another, it is important to take a closer look at the community foundation option.

PART FOUR

The Community Foundation Option

As one type of traditional charity, the community foundation has the tax advantages of being publicly supported and does not have the disadvantages of being a private foundation. This section explains how the community foundation differs from other public charities and why it is an attractive option in a variety of circumstances.[22]

Community foundations do not have a separate, legal classification in the tax code. In almost every circumstance, community foundations are classified as traditional charities under Section 509(a)(1). However, their history goes back to 1914 and thus predates the tax code itself. The Council on Foundations defines a community foundation as a tax exempt, not-for-profit, autonomous, publicly supported philanthropic institution comprised primarily of permanent funds endowed by many separate donors for the long-term benefit of the residents of a defined geographic area. Even though community foundations do not have a separate legal classification, the Treasury regulations defining publicly supported organizations of the Traditional charity variety provide great detail about the rules governing community trusts or community foundations. In contemplating the possible formation of a new foundation focusing on local needs, one would be well advised to learn the advantages of utilizing an existing community foundation or creating a new one to service the local community.

Community foundations develop, receive and administer endowment funds from private sources and manage them under community control for charitable purposes primarily focused on local needs. Their grants normally are limited to charitable organizations within a specific identified region or local community, and their charitable giving and other charitable activities are overseen by a board of directors representing the diversity of community interests. Originally conceived as a vehicle primarily for those desiring to leave property by will in perpetuity, community foundations have broadened their range over the years to accept more lifetime and short-term gifts.

Community foundations have two major purposes: to seek funds from private sources to build a pool of permanent capital for local philanthropic purposes, and to allocate and distribute such funds for public needs.

---

[22] Hoyt, Christopher, *Legal Compendium for Community Foundations*, Council on Foundations, Washington, D.C. (1996). This publication provides a thorough description of all the legal rules applicable to community foundations.

Developers of a Capital Pool for Philanthropy

A community foundation attracts capital in ways not intended to impede the efforts of local service organizations to raise annual operating support. It is a supplement to federated funds and other agencies, not a competitor. It seeks its resources from testators, living donors, business corporations, other nonprofit organizations, trade associations, clubs and occasionally from units of government.

In bringing resources into a pool, the community foundation enhances the utility of each fund by developing an endowment of a size that is better equipped to tackle community problems. By pooling resources, a community foundation can support one joint staff (as opposed to different staffs for each fund) and can take advantage of the obvious economies of scale.

Distributors of Funds for Philanthropy

Having drawn capital resources together, a community foundation distributes funds as its governing body determines or to charitable agencies and fields of interest designated by donors at the time of making their gifts. Its staff, supported by pooled resources, can become well acquainted with the emerging and changing needs of the local community, and thus provides professional expertise not always available to private donors, corporations, unstaffed private foundations and other grantmakers. The permanence of a community foundation ensures the ongoing presence of such expertise, and the public structure of both its governing body and its procedures ensures that its grantmaking choices are responsive to community needs.

Since the formation of the first community foundation in Cleveland in 1914, this type of institution has grown in popularity around the nation. In 1997, there were more than 400 community foundations with assets ranging from a few thousand dollars to over $1 billion. Together, community foundations hold assets in excess of $13 billion and distribute annually more than $900 million. In addition to the main purpose just outlined, each community foundation has certain basic characteristics in common, as summarized here.

Form

Community foundations are created as trusts or nonprofit corporations whose charitable distributions are made by a distribution committee in the trust form, or by a board of directors in the corporate form. In the trust form, banks or other investment firms serve as trustees under a common governing instrument that may be executed using similar language by each local institution that agrees to accept funds constituting a part of that community's foundation. In some communities, one bank serves as sole trustee; but in most areas, a number of institutions with trust powers accept funds under the declaration of trust of their community's foundation. In the trust form, banks or other institutions, as trustees, manage the investment function; a distribution committee or board of directors manages the distribution function. In the nonprofit corporation form, the board of directors often performs both functions.

Geography and Size

A community foundation operates primarily to serve a chosen area, but on occasion it may accept funds for distribution outside that area. Generally, each community foundation serves an area of natural cohesion whether it be a city, greater metropolitan area, county or state. While no specific minimum geographic size is required, the smaller the population, the fewer number of potential donors and corporations likely to be available to provide the basic support.

Governing Body

The Treasury regulations governing many community foundations require that all the combined or pooled funds (component parts) be subject to a common governing body or distribution committee which directs or, in the case of a fund designated for specified beneficiaries, monitors the distribution of all of the funds exclusively for charitable purposes. The governing body must represent the broad interests of the public rather than the personal or private interests of a limited number of donors. Community foundations frequently satisfy this public representation requirement by filling positions on the governing body with: (1) public officials, (2) members appointed by public officials, (3) persons with special knowledge in a particular field or discipline in which the community foundation operates, and/or (4) community leaders such as corporate executives, educators or civic leaders.

Range of Service to Donors

Community foundations provide a variety of ways to respond to the needs of donors whether the gifts are permanent or short-term. **Unrestricted funds** are most sought after by community foundations because they provide the governing body with the maximum amount of flexibility to respond to the most pressing needs of the community. **Designated funds** are created by the donor *at the time of transferring the assets*, and specifically name the agency or agencies to receive the benefit of the fund. **Donor-advised funds** are created by the donor, reserving at the time of making the gift, the privilege (from time to time thereafter) to recommend agencies to receive grants. However, the ultimate power to make all grant decisions must lie with the governing body and such recommendations can be redirected. **Field-of-interest funds** are established by a donor by specifying at the time of asset transfer some broadly identified field of charitable concern. Examples would be health, education or cultural arts. In any of the various funds noted above, a donor can name the fund thereby providing an opportunity to give his or her family name a place in the philanthropic history of the community. Community foundations normally charge a fee for these donor services, often based on a percentage of the value of the corpus of the fund.

Variance Power

Treasury regulations for many community foundations require that the governing body have a variance power. Specifically, the rule states that the governing body has the power (alone or with court approval) "to modify any restriction or condition on the distribution of funds for any specified charitable purposes or to specified organizations if in the sole judgment of the governing body . . . such restriction or condition becomes, in effect, unnecessary, incapable of fulfillment, or inconsistent with the charitable needs of the community or area served." The concept of including a variance power in the design of a community foundation has been present since the first one was formed in Cleveland. In fact, providing a variance power was a major reason for starting a community foundation since it provided a reasonable mechanism to avoid having the donor's restriction become obsolete or impossible to fulfill (sometimes called the rule of the dead hand).

The size and number of community foundations in the United States is growing steadily. Additional reasons why a donor might choose to establish a fund at a community foundation are provided in part five.

PART FIVE

Choosing the Right Type of Foundation

Up to this point, the reader has been introduced to some basic elements of tax law governing exempt charitable organizations with a special emphasis on the significant differences between public charities and private foundations. In addition, this book has examined rules governing the operation of three types of public charity, six types of private foundation and the community foundation option. It may be crystal clear at this point which type of foundation best suits the reader's purposes; however, if the best choice is still in doubt, this part is intended to sharpen the focus. Here is a review course of what has gone before—but with a new slant to it. What follows is a summary description of *why* the founder of a foundation might choose one type over another. The reader should keep in mind that more than one option may be suitable for his or her purposes. It may require thorough review with legal counsel to choose the preferred option but at least you should be well prepared for that important consultation.

A Word About Size

Before turning to the many reasons why a prospective donor might pick one type of foundation over another, it may be helpful to say a word about minimum size. Often the question is asked: How much is needed to start a foundation? At what point does a donor have enough resources to create a separate grantmaking organization rather than make direct gifts to existing charities or establish a fund with a community foundation? There really is no universally acceptable rule of thumb.

A free-standing grantmaking organization with paid staff and necessary legal and accounting fees obviously is going to cost more than one with no paid staff, an active volunteer board and pro bono services from an accountant and an attorney. One must determine the amount of funds likely to be available for spending annually, and then ask what amount will be left for grants after paying for necessary administrative costs.

In performing this analysis, two important factors should be considered in determining the feasibility of starting a new foundation. First, how broad or narrow is the purpose of the foundation? A narrow, single-purpose foundation can obviously be successful with fewer resources. A broad, multi-purpose foundation will clearly require more administrative expense. Secondly, can the proposed new foundation accomplish its purpose effectively and efficiently while employing good standards in its operations? In 1980 the Council on Foundations approved several "Principles and Practices for Effective Grantmaking" (see pp. 93-94). Among other issues, these recommendations note the importance of open communication with the public and responsiveness to grantseekers. The long-term health and independence of the philanthropic field depends on maintaining a positive relationship with government and the public. Responsible grantmaking is an important factor in maintaining a positive public view of philanthropy.

In short, the question of size boils down to this: can the new foundation accomplish its purpose given the resources available to it while employing responsible procedures?

The Public Charity (or Public Foundation) Options

There are a number of reasons why those starting foundations might prefer to choose one of the public charity options. As noted earlier, Congress has favored the organization that, in concept at least, is actively providing charitable services directly rather than storing its gifts away in an endowment and using only the income to make grants to others. All the public charity options share the following characteristics in common:

- They are *not* liable for any excise tax on their net investment income.

- They are *not* subject to most of the stricter operational rules and requirements of private foundations which can result in the imposition of penalty taxes on activities such as:

    1. Acts of self-dealing, broadly defined.

    2. Failure to meet a minimum distribution or payout rule.

    3. Failure to divest controlling interest in any business.

    4. Investment of assets in ways that jeopardize the carrying out of their exempt purpose.

    5. Making certain types of expenditures to individuals, to non-charitable organizations or for voter registration purposes without following specific guidelines.

    6. Making any expenditures for non-charitable purposes.

- However, they are subject to intermediate sanction penalties.

- They *may* use (an insubstantial) part of their annual expenditures for lobbying consistent with their exempt purposes.

- Their living donors may take advantage of the most liberal charitable deduction rules available.

- They can own all or a substantial portion of a business concern, especially one given by a donor, although there may be a tax on unrelated business income.

In addition to factors listed immediately above which are common to all public charities, the following are some additional reasons why a foundation founder might choose one type of public charity classification over another.

The Traditional Charity[23]—Section 509(a)(1)

In choosing this form of organization, the donor is likely to feel comfortable with several expectations. Not all of the four characteristics listed here are vital to the choice of the Traditional charity, but if one or more are true, this option is a likely candidate:

- Regular contributions or grants are expected from a large number of sources (e.g., individuals, corporations, private foundations, governments).

- No significant portion of revenue is likely to come from gross receipts (sales, admissions, fees for service, etc.)

- On a constant basis, the organization can meet the public support test through regular contributions sufficient to make up at least one-third of its support; in the alternative (should the one-third test not be met), the composition of the organization's board and other characteristics will be sufficiently public, and the organization can meet an absolute minimum public support test equal to at least ten percent of all support.

- The organization intends and expects to build up an endowment that will produce more than one-third of its regular support. Endowment building is not a requirement; but, if endowment income will exceed one-third of support, the gross receipts option (below) will not work.

The Gross Receipts Charity[24]—Section 509(a)(2)

Less common than the traditional charity, the Gross Receipts charity is likely to have the following characteristics:

- The organization expects to receive a substantial portion of its revenue from gross receipts (e.g., dues, admissions, sales, fees for services) paid in by a wide number of members, customers, clients or patrons.

---

[23] See p. 7.
[24] See p. 11.

- If the gross receipts alone are not likely to provide one-third of the regular support, the organization regularly expects to receive contributions from a wide number of sources (individuals, corporations and private foundations that are not disqualified persons plus government agencies), which, when added to the gross receipts, will satisfy the absolute minimum one-third public support test.

- The organization does not expect to build up a significant endowment such that more than one-third of its support would constitute endowment income.

The Supporting Organization[25]—*Section 509(a)(3)*

Although the rules for qualifying as a supporting organization are complicated, this option has demonstrated broad flexibility and has been adapted to a multitude of different situations. Its unique feature is that it avoids all the rules governing private foundations and yet it is not required to meet a public support test. Its major drawback is that some donor control must be relinquished to the organizations it supports. Listed below are several characteristics often present when this option is chosen:

- The donor often is still alive (or is an active corporation) and wishes to take an active role in running the foundation.

- The donor is prepared to provide an initial endowment or make sufficient annual contributions.

- The donor wishes to take advantage of the most liberal charitable deduction rules available.

- The donor does not want to be saddled with the need to meet a public support test requiring constant fundraising.

- The donor wishes to avoid the restrictions applicable to private foundations.

- In return for the above, the donor is willing to give up some degree of control to the supported organizations chosen.

- Occasionally, the donor wishes to endow the foundation with all or a substantial share of the ownership in a business (frequently one that is closely held by the family).

---

[25] See p. 12.

The Community Foundation[26]

As detailed in part four, the community foundation is an attractive option in a variety of circumstances. In almost every case, the community foundation will be classified as a traditional charity; more technically, the IRS will have approved its Section 509(a)(1) status. Consequently, it will have all the same favorable characteristics noted above for this type of public charity. In addition, other reasons might be considered in creating a fund with a community foundation.

- Rather than making a one-time gift to a specific charity, the donor prefers to make a lasting, permanent gift that will benefit a specific geographic area to which he or she is particularly attached (e.g., home town, county, metropolitan area or state) or that will benefit a particular type of charity or field of interest within that geographic boundary *that does not require* permanent commitment to a specific agency.

- Whether by lifetime gift or bequest after death, the donor wishes to avoid creating another institution with another set of administrative overhead requirements and expenses. Instead, the donor is attracted to the existing, experienced staff already in place at the community foundation where economies of scale are present.

- Where an endowed gift is intended, the amount of the gift is unlikely to sustain separate, independent staffing and administration without significantly reducing its grantmaking capacity.

- The donor has a strong desire to be certain the restrictions on his or her gift do not become obsolete (the rule of the dead hand). If the initial gift or established fund is limited through certain specifications or charitable designations reflecting the donor's preferences, the donor is attracted by the community foundation's variance power which permits its governing board to alter the restrictions of the gift to fit changing circumstances without the need for costly court procedures.

- Small existing *private* foundations may find that the burden of administrative costs necessary for compliance with federal tax law and state corporate or trust law significantly impedes their impact. Transferring their assets to a community foundation can be an attractive and viable option.

- Similarly, for-profit companies with growing charitable contributions programs may lack the needed expertise to direct their gifts for maximum impact on the community. In addition, they may not wish to develop that capacity in their own staff. The community foundation may provide the appropriate answer.

---

[26] See pp. 35-38.

- Speed also may be an advantage to the donor. Because the legal apparatus is already in place, an existing community foundation will have appropriate forms available so that the donor may literally establish the fund and take advantage of tax deductions in one visit.

The Private Foundation Options

Despite the advantages of creating a public charity or using a community foundation, the advantages of forming a private foundation can outweigh other factors in a number of circumstances. In most cases where the private foundation is the preferred option, two major factors are present. First, the founder often wishes to maintain the maximum independence and control to use the funds in an innovative, responsive or possibly controversial way. And, second, the founder is not particularly concerned or worried about the added restrictions placed on private foundations (paying an excise tax, making a minimum payout, not self-dealing, not owning a business, not making jeopardizing investments, not lobbying, etc.).

While contributions to the private foundation during lifetime may be more limited in their deductibility, the donor may intend to delay the major endowment gift until death at which time the limitations disappear. In fact, since the Tax Reform Act of 1969, many large private foundations have received the bulk of their endowments by bequest. Private foundation endowments also have been established through other means such as the sale of major medical institutions or court ordered settlements in toxic waste or environmental suits. Each type of private foundation option, nevertheless, has certain characteristics that make it particularly attractive in comparison to others.

The Independent Foundation[27]

By far the most common private foundation option, this option is chosen when either a significant endowment is available, or a living donor (or small group of donors) is prepared to make annual contributions. Most family foundations utilize this option. In addition, some or all of these factors are likely to be present:

- A donor with sufficient resources in hand wishes to pursue or advance certain values or philanthropic ends that are not represented or served in any other way, or at least not in the donor's community.

- The donor wishes to instill in his or her children and other family members the value of philanthropic giving so that it may be passed on to other generations and serve as a binding force for the family (note that this goal can also be accomplished with a fund at a community foundation).

---

[27] See p. 27.

- The size of the endowment is large enough to support separate professional staff, or the endowment is sufficient to cover the necessary legal and accounting fees, and the foundation is prepared to operate without employed staff using volunteer directors or trustees.

- Rather than create a major endowment, a donor may wish to use the private foundation vehicle as a means for evening out annual charitable contributions to his or her favorite charities by building up a small endowment in high income years to balance out years with lower income.

- The founder envisions no need for additional public support (the endowment is sufficient, or regular commitments are in place from a single or small group of donors). Moreover, the founder wishes to avoid the constant burden of fundraising to meet any public support test.

The Company-Sponsored Foundation[28]

Legally, the company foundation is identical completely to the independent foundation. In fact, the IRS and the tax code do not use the term company foundation and do not distinguish between the two in any way. In practice, however, the main difference is, of course, the nature of the founder. Here the founder is an existing for-profit corporation that usually has one or more of the following characteristics:

- A significant corporate contributions program is already in place.

- A desire to reorganize the company's charitable giving approach, or to provide a more visible, concentrated focus to a company's charitable grantmaking.

- A desire to provide a steady level of charitable giving in low-profit years, as well as in high-profit years by building a reserve in the foundation during good years. While building up the endowment, the company can still obtain current year tax deductions (a company can deduct up to ten percent of pre-tax income for charitable contributions annually).

- The company is not worried about the minimum payout rule, since annual company cash contributions flowing through the foundation will more than meet the requirement (five percent of investment assets usually is small, since endowments rarely exceed one or two years of giving).

---

[28] See pp. 27-28. See also Coy, John F., *When Corporate Foundations Make Sense*, Council on Foundations, Washington, D.C. (1994).

- For similar reasons, the company is not concerned about the two-percent excise tax on investment income, since such income will be limited based on a small (or no) endowment.

- The need for additional staff or administrative expenses is minimal because the staff is already administering the corporate giving program, and necessary legal or accounting assistance readily is available in existing corporate departments.

- A desire to make grants to charities overseas, and the corporation cannot obtain a charitable deduction by making such gifts directly through its corporate giving program.[29]

- A desire to shield the chief executive officer and other top corporate officials from charitable solicitations by requiring prospective donees to work directly through the company foundation following its application procedures.

The Conduit or Pass-Through Foundation[30]

Because the tax laws favor making large charitable gifts after death (estate tax deductions) rather than during lifetime (income tax deductions), many living donors favor using the conduit foundation option during lifetime to get the foundation established. Then, upon death, the foundation becomes fully funded and no longer functions as a conduit but rather as an endowed private foundation. Several other advantages may also be desired:

- The donor wishes to maintain maximum available private control *and still take advantage of the most liberal rules* limiting the deductibility of charitable contributions. Because the gifts flow through the foundation, the most liberal rules apply.

- Either the donor is not interested in building a large endowment, or can wait until death when it can be established by bequest.

- Deductible gifts made to the foundation can be used (within limits) to pay foundation staff. If the donor pays the staff directly, the payments would not qualify as charitable contributions.

- Once a conduit foundation is established, the donor may decide for a given year not to be a conduit and use that year to meet the minimum payout rule (which would be minimal) and apply the excess to building up some endowment.

---

[29] Edie, John A., *Beyond Our Borders: A Guide to Making Grants Outside the U.S.*, Council on Foundations, Washington, D.C. (1994), 63 pp.

[30] See p. 28.

- In some cases, the donor may wish to avoid the pressure of deciding on all necessary charitable donees late in December after he or she has determined how much money is available for charitable giving. Use of the conduit foundation provides the donor with two and one-half more months (but a regular private foundation provide an additional 12 months).

The Pooled Common Fund[31]

In most respects, the pooled common fund option is similar to the conduit foundation (see above). Although, it is technically classified as a private foundation and subject to the private foundation rules, contributions to it also may be deducted using the most liberal rules available. However, it is not possible to establish a permanent endowment since all the corpus of the fund must be paid out within a year of the donor's death (the corpus may be paid upon death to a donor-advised fund within a community foundation which provides for successor advisors). In addition, unlike the conduit foundation, the donor cannot change the classification of the private foundation from year to year. The governing instrument of a pooled common fund must require the distributions of income annually and the distributions of corpus after death. Therefore, donors choosing this option are likely to have the following purposes in mind:

- Retaining total control over which public charities will receive grants.

- Desiring not to create a permanent endowment after death.

- Obtaining the right to use the most liberal rules governing charitable deductions despite retention of control.

- Establishing a larger combination of funds—by pooling funds with other family members or other donors—in order to reduce investment and administrative expenses.

- Regulating the donor's annual giving levels. With larger gifts to the fund in high income years, donors can more easily retain a steady level of giving overall.

- Providing a future source of major gifts in years when donors may—for tax purposes—not wish to give from personal taxable income.

---

[31] See pp. 28-29.

The Operating Foundation[32]

The distinguishing characteristic of an operating foundation—that it directly and actively uses the bulk of its income to provide a charitable service or run a charitable program—rather than to make grants to others for similar purposes.

Although operating foundations are private foundations and are regulated by most of the stricter set of rules, gifts to them by living donors receive the most liberal treatment applicable to charitable contributions. Some or all of the following factors are present when forming an operating foundation:

- Substantial assets are available to form an endowment, or one donor will make regular contributions.

- The desired intent is to operate directly some charitable service or activity.

- The founder either prefers not to worry about constantly meeting a public support test, or fears the inability to meet it.

- Occasionally, no endowment is available but a limited number of substantial donors are committed to supporting the foundation. However, the number of annual contributors is so limited that meeting a public support test is not possible. Direct operation of a charitable activity is still the intent.

- Where a limited number of living donors are involved, the most liberal charitable deduction rules will be desired.

The Exempt Operating Foundation[33]

The classification known as the exempt operating foundation is not a viable option for those exploring the formation of a new foundation. In creating this option in 1984, Congress specifically limited the eligibility requirements so as to prevent newly formed organizations from seeking this classification. This type of classification is available only in two circumstances: (1) an organization that was classified as an operating foundation on January 1, 1983, and has maintained that classification since that date; or (2) an organization that has met the public support test for a traditional charity or a Gross Receipts charity for ten years.

It is now time to turn to the legal mechanics of establishing a foundation. As a handy reference to the differing treatment of the types of foundations available, the reader should review the following comparison charts.

---

[32] See pp. 29-31.
[33] See pp. 32-33.

Public Foundations: Effects of Selected Tax Laws

Laws Affecting Living Donors	Traditional Charity	Gross Receipts Charity	Supporting Organization	Community Foundation
Cash Gift	50% AGI	50% AGI	50% AGI	50% AGI
Appreciated Property	30% AGI	30% AGI	30% AGI	30% AGI
Carryover Available	5 years	5 years	5 years	5 years
Value of Appreciated Property	Fair Market Value	Fair Market Value	Fair Market Value	Fair Market Value

Laws Affecting Deceased Donors

All Gifts	No Limits	No Limits	No Limits	No Limits

Laws Affecting Organization

Investment Tax	No	No	No	No
Self-Dealing Tax	No	No	No	No
Payout Requirement	No	No	No	No
Tax on Excess Holdings	No	No	No	No
Jeopardy Investment Tax	No	No	No	No
Tax on Certain Grants [a]	No	No	No	No
Public Support Test	Yes	Yes	No	Yes
Public Inspection on Tax Return [b]	For 3 Years After Filing	For 3 Years After Filing	For 3 Years After Filing	For 3 Years After Filing
Intermediate Sanctions	Yes	Yes	Yes	Yes

(a) Political campaign expenditures and excess lobbying by any public foundation are subject to penalty tax.

(b) In addition to public inspection, public charities will be required to provide take home copies at a reasonable cost when requested. This requirement is expected to go into effect in late 1998.

AGI = Adjusted Gross Income

Private Foundations: Effects of Selected Tax Laws

Laws Affecting Living Donors	Independent Foundation	Company Foundation	Conduit Foundation	Pooled Common Fund	Operating Foundation	Exempt Operating Foundation
Cash Gifts	30% AGI	10% Taxable Income (Corp.) 30% AGI (Ind.)	50% AGI	50% AGI	50% AGI	50% AGI
Appreciated Property	20% AGI	10% Taxable Income (Corp.) 20% AGI (Ind.)	30% AGI	30% AGI	30% AGI	30% AGI
Carryover Available	5 years	5 years	5 years	5 years	5 years	5 years
Value of Appreciated Property	FMV for Publicly Traded Stock*; Otherwise, Cost Only	FMV for Publicly Traded Stock*; Otherwise, Cost Only	Fair Market Value	Fair Market Value	Fair Market Value	Fair Market Value

Laws Affecting Deceased Donors

	Independent Foundation	Company Foundation	Conduit Foundation	Pooled Common Fund	Operating Foundation	Exempt Operating Foundation
All Gifts	No Limits	No Limits	No Limits	No Limits	No Limits	No Limits

Laws Affecting Organization

	Independent Foundation	Company Foundation	Conduit Foundation	Pooled Common Fund	Operating Foundation	Exempt Operating Foundation
Investment Tax	2% or 1%	2% or 1%	2% or 1%	2% or 1%	2% or 1%	No
Self-Dealing Tax	Yes	Yes	Yes	Yes	Yes	Yes
Payout Requirement	5% of Assets	5% of Assets	All Gifts Plus Income	All Income	Varies	Varies
Tax on Excess Holdings	Yes	Yes	Yes	Yes	Yes	Yes
Jeopardy Investment Tax	Yes	Yes	Yes	Yes	Yes	Yes
Tax on Certain Grants	Yes	Yes	Yes	Yes	Yes	Yes
Public Support Test	No	No	No	No	No	No
Public Inspection on Tax Return	For 180 Days After Filing	For 180 Days After Filing	For 180 Days After Filing	For 180 Days After Filing	For 180 Days After Filing	For 180 Days After Filing
Intermediate Sanctions	No	No	No	No	No	No

* Subject to possible change by Congress, FMV deductibility for gifts of publicly traded stocks expires June 30, 1998.

AGI = Adjusted Gross Income; **FMV** = Fair Market Value; **Corp.** = Corporation; **Ind.** = Individual

First Steps in Starting a Foundation

PART SIX

First Steps in Starting a Foundation

Readers who have studied the previous pages should now have a better idea about which type of charitable organization is most appropriate to meet their objectives. As shown, the advantages and disadvantages of each type of organization vary greatly. To begin actual formation without knowing where you want to come out is foolhardy. However, once you have determined which charitable organization vehicle is best suited to your needs, the actual mechanics of creating a legal, tax-exempt entity are straightforward. The hard part is completed; you have become familiar with the important differences between public charities and private foundations and have made the proper selection. What is the next step?

If, by this point, the first meeting with legal counsel has not occurred, make that appointment. By studying this book, you should have saved time and legal fees. In addition, by studying this part (and the appropriate documents in the appendix) you will be well prepared to provide all the necessary information to the attorney, thus making the attorney's job easier and reducing the costs of creating the foundation. One should note that the legal fees incurred in establishing the foundation are legitimate expenses, and, assuming the fees are reasonable, may be applied in meeting the minimum payout requirement for private foundations.

Trust or Corporation?

Perhaps the first decision that needs to be made in starting a foundation is what legal form should be used. Should it be a trust or a not-for-profit corporation? In past years, the more popular choice was the trust, but recently, the corporate form has predominated. There is general consensus today that the corporate form is more flexible and adaptable to most foundation purposes. It should be emphasized that whatever form one chooses, it will be specifically regulated by state law, not federal law. Each jurisdiction has its own set of statutes which set out the rules for forming and running both a trust and a not-for-profit corporation. While a great deal of uniformity exists among state laws, each state has its own particular requirements to some extent. It makes little difference whether an organization is formed under one state's law or another's. However, this issue is another area where your legal counsel becomes indispensable.

The Trust Option

Generally speaking the requirements for a trust are less formal, both in formation and in operation. In most states, there will be few or no requirements for regular meetings, minutes, state filings, officers or other recordkeeping requirements. However, amending the charitable trust instrument may be more difficult possibly requiring court approval and notice to the state attorney general. Depending on state law or on how the trust instrument is drafted, replacing a trustee or providing for successor trustees may also be more difficult. The trust form (while lacking certain formal requirements) often is more rigid and harder to adapt to changing circumstances that are likely to occur over time.

In some states, trustees are restricted in how much authority they can delegate to others. Generally, trustees can delegate authority to one trustee and they can employ agents to perform ministerial tasks; but they sometimes cannot delegate discretionary authority (investment or grant selection decisions). In short, more direct involvement may be required of trustees than may be *required* of corporate directors.

In some states, trusts will not be required to file annual reports with the attorney general (or similar official) that may be an advantage. However, even though state law may not require regular meetings and minutes, many lawyers and certified public accountants will insist on such a practice; and frequently minutes of the organization's meetings often are the first item reviewed by IRS agents in the audit of a charitable organization.

The Corporate Option

The corporate approach is more formal both in its creation and in its operational requirements. Articles of incorporation, bylaws, regular meetings, minutes, state filings and other reporting requirements are necessary in most states. Filing fees usually accompany each state filing requirement. But, as noted above, these more formal requirements may be an advantage since keeping thorough records is simply a good practice and the first line of defense in maintaining the tax-exempt status of the organization if challenged by an IRS audit or by a similar examination by state officials.

Many states now require that an annual report be submitted to the attorney general (or other state agency) by each nonprofit organization over minimal size. In most cases, failure to submit this report may result in involuntary dissolution of the organization.

Despite these formal requirements, the nonprofit corporation often provides greater protection from personal liability for the directors (see discussion of fiduciary duty below). The corporate form also provides greater advantages in its adaptability to changing circumstances. Corporate bylaws can be drafted to facilitate amendments, and bylaws usually decide how directors and successor directors are selected. In short, the governing instruments of the corporation can be more readily altered to reflect the changing charitable needs of the community and the donor's charitable interests. For instance, donors who wish to maintain control of a charitable corporation but limit their own day-to-day involvement may name themselves members with the power to elect directors who then run the organization. Also, powers can easily be delegated to one or two board members or officers if permitted by the bylaws.

The corporate form has other advantages. Many states have crafted legislation clearly giving nonprofit corporations the right and obligation to indemnify officers and directors under specified circumstances. State laws with respect to indemnifying trustees of a trust are often less protective. Secondly, if the foundation expects to receive deductible donations from for-profit corporations the corporate form must be used. The Internal Revenue Code prohibits charitable trusts from using corporate contributions for grants to non-U.S. charities.

Other Considerations

Under most circumstances, the tax consequences of the trust versus the corporate form are identical. However, if the organization expects to have unrelated business income (income from a business having no relation to the exempt purpose of the organization), the tax on such income will differ. The tax on corporations will generally be higher.

The question is often raised, who has the higher fiduciary duty—charitable trustee or corporate director? Traditionally, the trustee has been held to a higher standard, although defining the standard for each progressively has become harder. More significantly, there appear to be different trends in different states. In a growing number of states, nonprofit corporate directors (but not trustees) are often protected—in areas other than self-dealing—if they act in reliance on advisors they believe to be competent, even if the advice (e.g., program, legal, accounting or investment) turns out to be incorrect.

Finally, many states have passed the Uniform Management of Institutional Funds Act (UMIFA) which provides welcome flexibility and protection to directors of non-profit corporations in managing investments. UMIFA rarely applies to trusts.

Tax-Exempt Status: State Level

As mentioned above, whether one chooses the trust or the corporate form, the process will be governed by state law. Therefore, the first official step is to draft the organizational documents necessary to create a legal, separate tax-exempt entity at the state level.

The governing instruments of charitable trusts and corporations share many features in common.

1. **Purpose Clause.** Without doubt the most important part of any governing instrument is its purpose clause. Federal law requires that every charitable foundation be "organized and operated exclusively for religious, charitable, scientific, testing for public safety, literary, or educational purposes. . . ."[34] While some organizations adopt just these words in their broadest context, others will specify a more narrow intent. A narrow purpose may become obsolete and require alteration of the governing instrument, which may take time and require additional legal costs. Also, in many states, funds raised for one purpose may not be used for another purpose. A broad purpose clause, therefore, permits flexibility.

2. **Distribution on Dissolution.** Federal law requires that each charitable foundation contain in its governing instruments an indication of how the assets of the organization will be disbursed if the organization should go out of existence. All assets are forever dedicated to charitable purposes and cannot "inure to the benefit of" a private individual (see below). Therefore, most governing instruments direct the assets upon dissolution be distributed to specifically named qualifying charities or permit the directors or trustees to determine which charities will receive the assets.

3. **Private Inurement.** The governing instruments should state that no earnings of the organization will "inure" (be transferred) to the benefit of a private individual.

4. **Lobbying and Political Campaigns.** The language of the governing instrument should prohibit the carrying on of lobbying as a substantial part of the organization's activities (private foundations must include even stricter limitations in this area—see part two, pp. 19-20). Political campaigning must also be prohibited.

Different types of charitable organizations will have other requirements and here is where legal counsel can be most helpful. For example, a supporting organization must state in its purpose clause that it is organized for the benefit of one or more public charities or contain other language that meets the requirements of Code Section 509(a)(3). Similarly, all *private* foundations must include in their governing instruments the prohibitions of Code Section 508(e) in order to achieve federal tax-exempt status unless the IRS has, by ruling, agreed that the laws of the particular state of formation contain those prohibitions. The Section 508 restrictions forbid private foundations and their managers from engaging in any acts that would violate Sections 4941 through 4945 (see part two, pp. 17-20).

---

[34] Section 501(c)(3).

The Trust Agreement

Under the state law of the preferred jurisdiction, the reader will execute a trust agreement which will: (1) name the original trustee or trustees who usually are the creators of the trust; (2) state the charitable purposes of the trust; (3) establish guidelines for the administration and distribution of trust assets (including distribution on dissolution); (4) name the successor trustees or establish the process by which successor trustees will be selected; and (5) state the duration of the trust (how long it will exist).

> **Note:** A sample trust agreement for creating a private foundation is included in the appendix. You should review this example *with caution* because it is not necessarily applicable in every state and, of course, is designed for a *private* foundation and *not* for other types of grantmaking organizations.

Corporate Documents

As noted above, the organizational requirements for a not-for-profit corporation are more numerous and more formal. In most jurisdictions, the following four steps must be completed.

1. **Articles of Incorporation.** The first step in forming a nonprofit corporation is filing articles of incorporation with the secretary of state or other appropriate state office. What must be included in the articles will vary from state to state but generally these items are specified: (1) the name of the corporation; (2) the purposes of the corporation; (3) the name of the registered agent and the address of the registered office; (4) the names and addresses of the incorporators (a minimum number is usually required); (5) a provision for distribution of assets upon dissolution; and 6) a method for amending the articles.

> **Note:** A sample Articles of Incorporation is included in the appendix. The sample is not applicable in all states.

2. **Bylaws.** In concert with state law requirements, the function of the bylaws is to provide clear and specific guidelines for the daily operation of the corporation. For the most part, bylaws should not try to specify every action that may or may not be taken. Instead, they should spell out major actions and leave flexibility for other activities. Resolutions of the board of directors can provide more specific instructions, if needed. Generally, bylaws will provide the following: (1) whether the corporation will have members who select the directors (most do not); (2) the number of directors, how they will be chosen, removed and succeeded; (3) the title and number of the officers, how they are elected, how they are removed and their duties; (4) indemnification of officers and directors to make clear that indemnification is contemplated and to establish the rights of the individuals so entitled; and (5) procedures for amending the bylaws.

Note: Sample bylaws are included in the appendix. The example is *not necessarily applicable* in all states and must be adapted to fit each particular jurisdiction. Making sure that the bylaws conform to federal and state laws is essential, for those laws will prevail over the bylaws.

3. **Organizational Meeting.** Some form of initial organizational meeting will be required. Generally the following actions take place at such a meeting: (1) election of directors; (2) election of officers, (3) adoption of bylaws, (4) adoption of a corporate seal, (5) adoption of a resolution permitting the opening of appropriate bank accounts, plus signing of bank signature cards, (6) establishment of a fiscal year, and (7) the taking of minutes.

4. **Corporate Seal and Minute Book.** Many states require that each not-for-profit corporation have a corporate seal, and that each corporation have a notebook or binder designated as the minute book to include the articles (plus amendments), the bylaws (plus amendments) and the minutes of all meetings.

Often, the state will set forth its own specific form of articles of incorporation that must be used to create the nonprofit corporation. The corporation is officially created on the date the articles are stamped and approved. In most jurisdictions, it takes three to four weeks from date of submission of articles of incorporation until date of approval although a few states will approve documents much more quickly.

Many states have other filing requirements as well as filing fees (such as registration of fundraisers). Some states require registration statements and annual reports as well. Consult an attorney for specific requirements in the appropriate state. An organization in one state may qualify to do business in another state as a foreign organization.

Tax-Exempt Status: Federal Level

Virtually every charitable organization—whether public or private—will want to obtain recognition of exemption from federal income tax. To apply, the foundation must submit IRS Form 1023, titled "Application for Recognition of Exemption Under Section 501(c)(3) of the Internal Revenue Code" (see appendix, pp.97-131). If the Form 1023 is filed by the end of the 27th month after the organization commences its existence (for corporations, upon state approval of articles of incorporation; for trusts, upon execution of the trust documents), the tax-exempt status of the foundation when approved by IRS will be retroactive to the date of formation of the organization.

The Form 1023 requires that a conformed copy of the articles of incorporation (or the trust agreement) and signed bylaws be attached to the application. Thus, organizing at the state level obviously is the first step. However, for those anxious to obtain official federal status as soon as possible, the Form 1023 should be completed while awaiting official state approval, at which point the application can be submitted at once. Normally, it takes four to six months to obtain your IRS Letter of Determination, which recognizes tax-exempt status for the foundation.

To avoid unnecessary delays during IRS review, it is crucial that the application be as specific and detailed as possible. Even if the information provided seems complete, one can expect the IRS to request additional information and detail, thus delaying your final approval. Most new foundations when filing have not yet started any activities and they may not wish to begin until tax exemption has been approved. Nevertheless, it is important when filing to spell out, as best as one can, the intended purposes and activities of the foundation into the foreseeable future. It is perfectly acceptable to state that no activities have begun at the time of application.

For private foundations and for public charities, the Form 1023 must be available for public inspection during regular business hours. Any papers submitted in support of the application (including any letter or document issued by the IRS with respect to the application) must also be made available.

Note: Drafting those sections of Form 1023 that ask for a description of activities, purposes and a five-year projected budget can often best be done by the reader and thus save legal fees; the attorney may wish to edit and amend them, but an initial drafting will save time. The applicant organization will not be bound to the proposed budgets, but they should reflect a thoughtful estimate of the new organization's plans, expressing in numbers what the statement of purpose expresses in words.

Final v. Advance Rulings

When the IRS approves an application, it sends a tax determination letter, which specifies two findings: (1) that the organization is recognized as exempt from federal income tax under Section 501(c)(3); and (2) that it is, or is not, a private foundation as defined in Section 509.

Normally, the recognition of exemption under Section 501(c)(3) is a final determination but it is dependent upon the *actual* operations of the foundation. If the foundation does not operate in accordance with the representations made in its formal application, its tax-exempt status may be removed—even retroactively. Obviously, when the application is based on estimates of future income and hoped-for activities, the foundation is not making an iron-clad commitment. However, if managers of the foundation should contemplate major changes in purpose or direction—especially if such changes involve amending its organizational documents—they should consider informing the IRS of the changes in advance and requesting a private letter ruling whereby IRS will indicate that the foundation's tax status is not affected. The foundation must inform the IRS of any changes at the time of filing the annual tax return—Form 990 or Form 990-PF.

If the organization is classified as a private foundation, the determination letter on this point will normally be considered final—a so-called definitive ruling. However, if you initially are determined not to be a private foundation, this part of the ruling normally will be only an advance determination.

Advance ruling periods are particularly common with publicly supported organizations (Traditional and Gross Receipts charities). In applying for tax status, the charity will request a five-year ruling period as the time in which to obtain the required public support for qualification under the rules chosen. The initial ruling letter from the IRS will state that the IRS has determined the organization reasonably can be expected to be a publicly supported organization of the particular kind chosen and that the organization will be so treated during the advance ruling period.

Within 90 days after the end of the advance ruling period, the charity must communicate with to the IRS to demonstrate that it has met the requirements of the public support test applicable to it. If the charity fails to meet the support test by the end of the advance ruling period (and does not switch to some other charitable organization category), it is reclassified as a private foundation and will be liable for the private foundation's excise tax on investment income retroactive to the beginning of the foundation's first taxable year. However, in case of reclassification, individual donors (including private foundations) who have relied on the public charity status during the advance ruling period are protected.

Cumulative List (Publication 78)

Once a tax determination letter has been sent out to the foundation, the IRS—in due course—adds the name of the foundation to it *Cumulative List of Organizations Contributions to Which Are Deductible Under Section 170(c)*, also referred to as IRS Publication 78 (see list of references, pp. 61-71). The *Cumulative List* is not always accurate or current, but it is used frequently by private foundations and other potential donors as a primary source for identifying the tax status of organizations. It is worth the time to make certain the foundation's name is listed and accurately represented. The IRS also publishes occasionally in the *Internal Revenue Bulletin* the names of organizations that have lost their public charity status and have been reclassified as private foundations.

Other Federal Requirements

Power of Attorney. The attorney or accountant representing the foundation will probably wish to include with the submission of the Form 1023 application another form: IRS Form 2848, Power of Attorney. Filing this form enables the attorney to deal directly with the IRS on the client's behalf; otherwise, the IRS does not communicate with the attorney or accountant and communicates directly with the client. By obtaining the power of attorney, the legal counsel or the accountant will also make certain that duplicate copies of all correspondence from the IRS will be sent to him or her.

Employee Identification Number (EIN). Each charitable foundation must also apply for an employee identification number using IRS Form SS-4 (see appendix, pp. 97-131). This form may be filed with the IRS prior to the filing of the Form 1023 or may be attached to it and submitted at the same time.

Annual Information Returns (Form 990 or Form 990-PF). The annual information return required for public charities is the Form 990; for private foundations it is the Form 990-PF. The return is due four and one-half months after the close of the foundation's fiscal year. For foundations using a calendar year, the return is due on May 15.

Both forms require significant amounts of detail about the operation of the foundation, although the Form 990-PF is more demanding. Because of their length and frequent alteration by IRS, copies are not included in the appendix; however, in forming a foundation one would be wise to review what is required to complete these forms. Good recordkeeping and a knowledgeable accountant are recommended strongly.

For private foundations, the Form 990-PF must be available for public inspection during normal business hours for a period of 180 days after public notice in a newspaper of general circulation. Such notice must be published by the due date for filing the return and a copy of the notice must be attached to the return. The notice must include the telephone number of the foundation's principal office. The penalty for failure to file a complete return by the due date is $10 per day for each day the return is late, up to a maximum of $5,000.

For public charities, the requirement is similar. However, a public charity must make its Form 990 available for inspection for three years.[35] No newspaper notice is required. The charity is not required to make available for public inspection the name or address of any contributor to the organization.

The penalty for failure to file a complete and timely return is higher for public charities than for private foundations.[36] The penalty is $20 per day up to a maximum of $10,000 (or 5 percent of the organization's assets, whichever is less). For charities with assets in excess of $1 million, the penalty is $100 per day, up to a maximum of $50,000.

Employee Related Filings. If the foundation should decide to pay compensation to directors, officers, trustees or staff, it will be responsible for withholding, depositing, paying

---

[35] See page 23.
[36] See code section 6652(c)(1)(A).

and reporting federal income tax and social security (FICA). However, organizations classified under Section 501(c)(3) are generally not subject to the Federal Unemployment Tax (FUTA). Where the individual payee is an independent contractor rather than an employee, the foundation is required to report such payments using Form 1099. IRS auditors insist on the proper use of the Form 1099 and one should consult an attorney or an accountant for advice in this regard. Additional information is available from an IRS publication titled *Circular E: Employer's Tax Guide*.

Postscript

Despite what may strike you as an unending stream of technical detail, starting a foundation is not a burdensome task—especially in the hands of experienced legal counsel. The task is dramatically easier if the donor and his or her advisers are familiar with the basics of tax-exempt law presented by this book. And, remember, that a fund at an existing community foundation often can be made in one visit with minimal paperwork.

Throughout its programs and services, the Council on Foundations is committed to encouraging the growth of organized grantmaking. Hopefully, this book will help promote such growth. Additional materials are noted in the list of references and Council staff are prepared to provide additional assistance if needed.

LIST OF REFERENCES

General

Edie, John A. "Congress and Foundations: Historical Summary." In *America's Wealthy and the Future of Foundations*, Foundation Center (New York, 1987). In-depth summary of legislative history through 1985. Also available directly from the Council on Foundations as a booklet titled *Congress and Private Foundations: An Historical Analysis*.

Exempt Organizations Reports. Commerce Clearing House (Chicago, IL), three volumes. A three-hole binder, loose-leaf comprehensive compendium of law and regulations governing tax-exempt organizations, updated through mailings every two weeks and includes coverage of state laws. Also includes laws, regulations, recent court decisions, administrative rulings, proposed legislation and is indexed by subject. Designed for the lawyer or practitioner in the field.

Hopkins, Bruce R., *The Law of Tax-Exempt Organizations*. John Wiley and Sons (New York, 1992), Sixth Edition, 1184 pages. Comprehensive treatment of the law of tax-exempt organizations helpful to both the novice and the expert. Includes explanation of charitable organizations, private foundations, procedures for qualifying as a tax-exempt organization and unrelated business income.

Council on Foundations, *Foundation Management Report*, Eighth Edition. (Washington, DC, 1996), 291 pages. Biennial report details board compensation packages and fringe benefits packages provided by foundations. Examines board/staff composition, board service and various management topics. Survey results are presented by asset category and by foundation type (private, corporate and community).

Council on Foundations, 1996 *Grantmakers Salary Report*. (Washington, DC), 160 pages. Yearly report contains salary norms for private, corporate, community and public foundations.

Council on Foundations, *Trustee Orientation Resource*. (Washington, DC, 1993), 112 pages. This resource is designed to provide new foundation trustees with a basic understanding of their role and responsibilities. Includes articles on trustee duties and issues and a listing of materials new trustees should obtain from their foundation to help orient themselves.

Tarnacki, Duane L., *Establishing a Charitable Foundation in Michigan*. Council of Michigan Foundations (Grand Haven, 1989). Second edition with a 1992 supplement. Intended as a how-to book for lawyers, accountants and professional real estate planners, this publication provides a step-by-step guide for setting up public charities, community foundations and private foundations in Michigan. Subjects discussed include: reasons for creating a charitable foundation, the charitable foundation as an estate planning tool, limitations on deductibility of contributions, types of charitable foundations, differences in organizational form, organizational documents, taxes, private foundation operating restrictions, fiduciary duties and indemnification. Extensive appendix includes many documents such as articles of incorporation, bylaws, tax returns and federal forms.

Tax Exempt Organizations. Prentice-Hall, Inc. (Englewood Cliffs, NJ, 1988), two volumes. A three-hole binder, loose leaf comprehensive compendium of law and regulations governing tax-exempt organizations, kept current through monthly mailings. Includes law regulations, IRS rulings, court cases, proposed legislation, IRS forms and instructions. Designed for the lawyer or practitioner in the field.

Private and Family Foundations

Beckwith, Edward J., and Marshall, David (Baker & Hostetler), *Grants to Individuals by Private Foundations*, Council on Foundations, (Washington, DC, 1995), 147 pages. Analyzes the legal considerations and general IRS rules for all grants to individuals, scholarship grants and grants that are not for study or travel. Highlights both factors to consider before developing a program of grants to individuals and new legal developments.

Edie, John A., *Family Foundations & The Law: What You Need to Know*, Council on Foundations (Washington, DC, 1995), 76 pages. An essential tool for family members who are responsible for running a family foundation. This book outlines the legal concepts every foundation manager should know. More than 90 issues are addressed, ranging from rules for charitable deductions to rules against self-dealing.

Fraser, David R., "Of Lasting Duration: Building a Legacy with a Private Foundation," *Foundation News & Commentary* (January/February 1988), pages 25-29. Addresses some of the early decisions that will determine the type of foundation you start.

Freeman, David F. and the Council on Foundations, *The Handbook on Private Foundations*. (New York, 1991), 321 pages. Thorough volume which covers a wide range of topics from creating a foundation to the governance and administration of private foundations, investment rules and regulations and government regulations of foundations. Contains an extensive bibliography and appendices with useful memoranda, forms, applicable tax codes and regulations.

Harrison, Carter R., *Spending Policies and Investment Planning for Foundations: A Structure for Determining A Foundation's Asset Mix*, Council on Foundations (Revised Edition, Washington, DC, 1995), 52 pages. This book advises foundations on how to establish sound spending and investment policies in the current financial market.

The Family Foundation Library Series, Council on Foundations (Washington, DC 1997). Four volumes: Governance, Management, Family Issues and Grantmaking. A comprehensive collection of information and experiences from more than 200 family foundation trustees nationwide. A new, valuable source for insight into the workings of a family foundation.

Toll, Martha A., *Operating Basics for Small Foundations*, Council on Foundations (Washington, DC, 1992), 50 pages. An overview of the essential elements of foundation operations that help small foundations administer their trusts to the letter of the law and run an office efficiently. Includes examples of foundation mission statements, guidelines and annual reports. A practical reference lists libraries, information bureaus and national and regional associations.

White, Benjamin T., *Foundation Desk Reference: A Compendium of Private Foundation Rules*, Southeastern Council of Foundations (Atlanta, GA, 1991), 77 pages. A three-hole binder looseleaf summary of federal laws and regulations governing private foundations. Supplements will be available as changes in federal law occur.

Why Establish a Private Foundation? Southeastern Council of Foundations (Atlanta, GA, 1996), Revised Edition, 22 pages. Summarizes numerous reasons for forming a private foundation and outlines the process of grantmaking suggesting ongoing sources of assistance for grantmakers. Also discusses organizing and establishing a foundation, choosing foundation managers, reporting and recordkeeping, consolidating with other foundations and terminating a foundation.

Ylvisaker, Paul N., *Family Foundations Now—and Forever?*, Council on Foundations (Washington, DC, 1991), 21 pages. This monograph identifies successful models of operation for family foundations that vary from continuous and exclusive family control to the disappearance altogether of family participation. Examples offer ideas of how others can negotiate the process of intergenerational succession.

Corporate Grantmaking

Beckwith, Edward J., David L. Marshall and Theodore F. Rodriguez, *Company Foundations and the Self-Dealing Rules*, Council on Foundations (Washington, DC, 1993), 30 pages. Provides specific rules that corporate foundations can follow to avoid self-dealing infringements. Provides guidelines for what is safe and what is not. Includes an appendix with an executive summary and a technical analysis of the self-dealing rules.

Coy, John F., *When Corporate Foundations Make Sense*, Council on Foundations (Washington, DC, 1994), 24 pages. Gives an overview of corporate support, outlines the role of a corporate foundation and gives advice on establishing a corporate foundation. Also useful for those who have a foundation and want to rethink how it can be more effective.

Edie, John A., *Corporate Giving and the Law: Steering Clear of Trouble*, Council on Foundations (Washington, DC, 1992), 24 pages. Legal and regulatory problems are identified with short explanations on how to avoid dilemmas for both company and corporate giving programs.

Clark, Sylvia and Kate Dewey, *Organizing Corporate Contributions: Options and Strategies*, Council on Foundations (Washington, DC, 1996). This book is designed to help corporations that are in the process of formalizing their giving programs by addressing the following: organizational options; state and federal requirements; the role of planning; structural options; grantmaking basics; and communications.

Shannon, James A. (editor), *Corporate Contributions Handbook: Devoting Private Means to Public Needs*, Jossey-Bass, Inc. (San Francisco, CA, 1991), 440 pages. Presents insights of leaders in corporate philanthropy based on their hands-on experience. Explains how to administer a grantmaking program including meeting legal requirements, running a matching gift program and monitoring the progress of grants.

Smith, Hayden W., *To Have or Have Not: A Corporate Foundation*, Council for Aid to Foundations (New York, 1989), 14 pages. This report discussed the circumstances that favor the establishment of a corporate foundation.

Community Foundations

Beckwith, Edward J., and David Marshall (Baker & Hostetler) with John A. Edie and Robert Edgar, *Establishing an Advised Fund Program: A Summary of Legal and Management Issues*, Council on Foundations (Washington, DC, 1992), 64 pages. A guide to the legal requirements that govern advised funds and how community foundations may successfully navigate the law in establishing their own advised fund program.

Community Foundation Training Manuals, Council on Foundations (Washington, DC, 1990), each manual 55 pages. Six manuals designed to train new staff and board members. Covers the mission and history of community foundations, governance, management, resource development, grantmaking, communications and public relations.

Edie, John A., *How to Calculate the Public Support Test*, Council on Foundations (Washington, DC, 1989), 34 pages. An easy-to-use guide with step-by-step instructions to determine the public support test.

Hoyt, Christopher, *Legal Compendium for Community Foundations*, Council on Foundations (Washington, DC, 1996). A complete summary of the rules and regulations that govern the creation and operation of community foundations.

1994 *Investment Performance and Practices of Community Foundations*, Council on Foundations (Washington, DC, 1995), 58 pages. Includes information on the median rate of return, spending policies, portfolio structure and the use of outside consultants. Illustrated with numerous tables and graphs.

Operating Foundations

Edie, John A., "Guidance Memorandum to Operating Foundations, 1984 Tax Act: Exempt Operating Foundations," Council on Foundations (Washington, DC), January 14, 1985 memorandum, 5 pages. Sets forth guidelines for "exempt operating foundation" status and cases where this status is desirable.

Foote, Joseph, "Service Unlimited Operating Foundations Deliver a Dazzling Variety of Services, Often Incognito," (Part I), *Foundation News & Commentary* (July/August 1985), pages 10-19. "You Name It They Do It, Operating Foundations' Services are Boundless," (Part II), *Foundation News & Commentary* (September/October 1985), pages 14-25. Examines the role operating foundations play in the nonprofit sector.

Special Issues

Edie, John A., *Use of Fiscal Agents: A Trap for the Unwary*, Council on Foundations (Washington, DC, 1989), 13 pages. Alerts the reader to potential problems when using fiscal intermediaries. Complete explanation of the pertinent rules and regulations.

Edie, John A., *Foundations and Lobbying: Safe Ways to Affect Public Policy*, Council on Foundations (Washington, DC, 1991), 135 pp.

Edie, John A., *Beyond Our Borders: A Guide to Making Grants Outside the U.S.*, Council on Foundations (Washington, DC, 1994), 66 pp.

Internal Revenue Service Documents

Department of the Treasury, Internal Revenue Service, *Publication 78: Cumulative List of Organizations* (revised periodically), U.S. Government Printing Office (Washington, DC). While subject to error, this publication is intended to list every organization to which charitable contributions are deductible as described in Section 170(c) of the Internal Revenue Code; includes charities, private operating foundations, private foundations and others.

Department of the Treasury, Internal Revenue Service, P*ublication 557: Tax-Exempt Status for Your Organization* (revised periodically), U.S. Government Printing Office (Washington, DC). Covers procedures, rules and regulations for organizations seeking tax-exempt status under Section 501(a) of the Internal Revenue Code. Contains detailed information on the determination of private foundation status.

Department of the Treasury, Internal Revenue Service, P*ublication 558: Tax Information for Private Foundations and Foundation Managers* (revised periodically), U.S Government Printing Office (Washington, DC). Detailed explanation of tax provisions governing private foundations; contents cover filing requirements, tax on net investment income, taxes on self-dealing, taxes on jeopardizing investments, excess business holdings and other rules.

Regional Associations of Grantmakers

There are nearly 40 different regional associations and networks of grantmakers throughout the United States. These associations range from formal organizations with programs managed by a professional staff to informal networks of grantmakers that meet only occasionally. Regional associations may serve one city or metropolitan area, or they may serve an area that includes several states. Twenty-five of the largest associations have formed the Forum of Regional Associations of Grantmakers (the Forum).

Regional associations offer local information and programming on a variety of topics of interest to grantmakers. Some associations have materials that are particularly helpful to individuals and corporations in setting up a foundation. For more information on the regional association nearest you, please contact the Forum of Regional Associations of Grantmakers at 202/466-6512.

Affinity Groups

Affinity groups serve as separate and independent coalitions of grantmakers concerned with a certain issue, such as the environment. The number of affinity groups recognized by the Council on Foundations continues to grow as grantmakers seek to collaborate in more meaningful ways. The activities of affinity groups vary. Many produce newsletters, hold annual meetings and sponsor workshops. For a complete list of affinity groups, please contact the affinity groups services staff at the Council on Foundations.

The Foundation Center: Standard Publications

The Foundation Center is an independent national service organization established by foundations to provide an authoritative source of information on philanthropic giving. The Center gathers and disseminates information on private giving through its libraries, public service programs and publications. It maintains for free public use a nationwide network of library collections offering reference and educational services, as well as the most comprehensive collection of foundation and corporate giving materials in the United States available to the public. The Foundation Center, 79 Fifth Avenue, New York, NY 10003-3076, 212/620-4230, 800/424-9836 (for publication orders only). Website: www.fdncenter.org

The Foundation Directory. Each annual version contains entries for over 40,000 private and community foundations with at least $2 million in assets or $200,000 in annual giving. *The Foundation Directory Supplement* contains updated listings for all of the foundations that have had substantial changes in their entries during a calendar year. Published annually.

The Foundation Directory, Part 2, 5th Edition. Each annual edition covers over 5,000 mid-sized foundations that hold assets from $1 million to $2 million or with annual grant programs from $50,000 to $200,000.

Guide to U.S. Foundations, Their Trustees, Officers and Donors. Formerly known as the National Data Book of Foundations, it contains brief listings of more than 38,500 private, corporate, community and operating foundations in the 1996 edition. Foundations are listed by state and indexed by name.

The Foundation 1,000. Formerly known as *Source Book Profiles*, lists comprehensive descriptions of the largest 1,000 foundations based on total annual giving. Nearly 65 percent of all foundation dollars are granted by the foundations listed in the 1996/97 edition.

National Directory of Corporate Giving, 4th edition. Profiles over 2,600 corporate foundations and direct giving programs. Contains indexes of officers, donors, trustees, geographic area, types of support, subject area and type of business.

National Directory of Grantmaking Public Charities. Covers over 800 public charities that award grants to nonprofit organizations. Includes current fiscal information, purpose and activities statements, giving interests and limitations, information on formal giving programs, description of recently awarded grants, application information, names of key officials and chapter locations.

Program-Related Investments. Provides information which is needed to understand the uses of charitable investing: current perspectives from providers and recipients, crucial tips on how organizations have sought out and managed PRIs, a directory of leading PRI providers, examples of over 550 PRIs and more.

The Foundation Grants Index. The 1996 edition of this annual publications lists over 72,000 grants of $10,000 or more awarded by over 1,000 foundations. Grants are indexed by subject area, recipient, type of support, geographic area and grantor organization.

Grant Guides. Twenty-eight guides exist for many subject areas, including aging, higher education, minorities, arts and cultures, and many others. Each guide describes foundation grants of $10,000 or more.

The Foundation Center's User-Friendly Guide, Fourth Edition. Ideal for first-time grantseekers, this guide covers the terminology and resources used by professional fundraisers. This book contains practical advice on securing tax exemption; searching potential funders with the most recent fundraising directories; using online services and CD-Roms to gather data on potential grantmakers; writing grant proposals; and more.

Foundation Fundamentals, Fifth Edition. Teaches the reader how to form a successful grantseeking strategy. The latest edition is full of revised charts, worksheets and information on the most recent trends in the field.

Foundation Giving. Facts and figures on charitable giving by private, corporate and community foundations. Analyzes the latest philanthropic trends by foundations type, geographic area, assets size and fields of interest.

Professional Support Organizations for Nonprofits

American Association of Fund-Raising Counsel

A membership organization of professional fundraising consulting firms founded to establish ethical standards for the profession and to collect and disseminate facts about all types of donors and the institutions they support. Annually publishes *Giving* USA, a widely used statistical portrait of philanthropic giving in the United States. For more information, contact: American Association of Fund-Raising Counsel, 500 Fifth Avenue, New York, NY 10036, 212/354-5799.

Funding Information Center

Administers the management of Assistance Program Workshops which are designed for managers, staff and board members of nonprofit organizations. Workshops include proposal writing, dialogue with donors, producing fundraising films for nonprofit organizations, grassroots fundraising, strategic planning and funding sources. For more information, contact: Funding Information Center, 530 McCullough, San Antonio, TX 78215, 512/227-4333.

Independent Sector

Promotes the nonprofit sector by encouraging volunteerism and charitable giving. Publications include: *Profiles of Excellence, Achieving Success in the Nonprofit Sector, The Nonprofit Lobbying Guide: Advocating Your Cause and Getting Results and Ethics and the Nation's Voluntary and Philanthropic Community.* For more information, contact: Independent Sector, 1828 L Street, NW, Washington, DC 20036, 202/223-8100.

National Center for Family Philanthropy

Assists individuals and families to identify and sustain a philanthropic mission for the purpose of strengthening and expanding American giving. Provides direct technical assistance, seminars, publications and referrals to other resources in the field. Encourages philanthropic giving by individuals and families, promotes greater public understanding of individual and family philanthropy, and serves as a resource to the philanthropic infrastructure serving individuals and family donors. For more information, contact: National Center for Family Philanthropy, 1220 19th Street, NW, Suite 300, Washington, DC 20036, 202/293-3424.

National Center for Nonprofit Boards

Helps nonprofit trustees and executives through publications, workshops and conferences. Their nationwide information center provides technical assistance for nonprofit board members. For more information, contact: National Center for Nonprofit Boards, 2000 L Street, NW, Washington, DC 20036, 202/452-6262. Website: http://www.ncnb.org

National Charities Information Bureau

Provides reporting and advisory service about national and international fundraising and nonprofit organizations that solicit contributions from the public. Purposes are to maintain sound standards in the field of philanthropy and to aid wise giving through advisory reports to contributors. For more information, contact: The National Charities Information Bureau, 19 Union Square West, 6th Floor, New York, NY 10003, 212/929-6300. Website: www.give.org

National Office on Philanthropy and the Black Church

Promotes collaboration between grantmakers and black church leaders interested in community revitalization. Educates grantmakers interested in enhancing the quality of life in the African American communities. Provides direct technical assistance, seminars, publications and referrals to other resources in the field. For more information, contact: The National Office on Philanthropy, 1090 Vermont Avenue, NW, Suite 1100, Washington, DC 20005, 202/789-3530.

National Society of Fund-Raising Executives

A membership organization that trains and educates development staff, association executives and other fundraising professionals in the art of fundraising. For more information, contact: National Society of Fund-Raising Executives, 1101 King Street, Suite 3000, Alexandria, VA 22314, 703/684-0410. Website: http://www.nsfre.org

Philanthropic Advisory Service of the Council of Better Business Bureaus

Sets standards for charitable solicitation and issues information on thousands of nationally soliciting organizations. This service routinely develops information and issues reports on national charitable organizations that are the subject of recent inquiries. For more information, contact: Philanthropic Advisory Service of the Council of Better Business Bureaus, 4200 Wilson Blvd., Arlington, VA 22203, 703/276-0100. Website: http://www.bbb.org/bbb/pas.html

Public Management Institute

Publishes *Corporate 500*, a directory of corporate grantmakers. Also provides other publications on fundraising and grantmaking, including *How To Get Corporate Grants*, *The Quick Proposal Workbook*, *Direct Mail Fund Raising*, *Budgeting For Nonprofits* and *How to Build a Big Endowment*. For more information, contact: Public Management Institute, 358 Brannan Street, San Francisco, CA 94107, 415/896-1900.

Society for Nonprofit Organizations

Provides a forum for the exchange of information, knowledge and ideas on strengthening and increasing productivity within nonprofit organizations and among their leaders. Maintains resource center of books, periodicals and tapes on operating an effective and efficient nonprofit organization. Also publishes *The Nonprofit World Journal*, a monthly magazine for nonprofits. For more information, contact: The Society for Nonprofit Organizations, 6314 Odana Road, Suite 1, Madison, WI 53719, 608/274-9777.

Support Center

Provides comprehensive management development services to hundreds of community organizations through its growing national network. Helps these organizations address their management needs through one-on-one consultation, tailor-made training programs and information referral services. For more information, or the regional office nearest you, contact: The Support Center, 2001 O Street, NW, Washington DC 20036, 202/833-0300.

Taft Group

Publishes numerous books on fundraising, corporate philanthropy, and individual giving. Titles include: *Corporate Giving Directory, America's New Foundations, Inside Japanese Support* and *The Nonprofit Computer Sourcebook*. Also produces newsletters on private and corporate foundation giving and fundraising. For more information, contact: The Taft Group, 835 Penobscot Building, Detroit, MI 48226-4094, 800/877-TAFT.

APPENDICES

> **Note:** The articles of incorporation presented here are not a model to copy; rather they are provided purely to illustrate what such a document might look like. Each state will have its own form or particular requirements to follow which may differ from state to state.

Sample Articles of Incorporation

The_____Foundation

We, the Incorporators, being natural persons of the age of twenty-one years or more and citizens of the United States, for the purpose of forming a corporation under the _____ Act of the State of _____, do hereby adopt the following Articles of Incorporation:

ARTICLE I

The name of the Corporation shall be the _____Foundation.

ARTICLE II

The purposes for which the Corporation is organized are:

1. The Corporation is organized exclusively for charitable, religious, literary, scientific and educational purposes as set forth in Section 501(c)(3) of the Internal Revenue Code including, for such purposes, the making of distributions to organizations that qualify as exempt organizations under Section 501(c)(3) of such Code.

2. No part of the net earnings of the Corporation shall inure to the benefit of, or be distributable to its directors, officers, or other private persons, except that the Corporation shall be authorized and empowered to pay reasonable compensation for services rendered and to make payments and distributions in furtherance of the purposes set forth in these Articles of Incorporation.

3. No substantial part of the activities of the Corporation shall include the carrying on of propaganda, or otherwise attempting to influence legislation (for private foundations, the language should read: "no part of the activities of the Corporation shall include the carrying on of propaganda or be used to influence legislation as defined in Section 4945), and the Corporation shall not participate in, or intervene in (including the publishing or distribution of statements) any political campaign on behalf of any candidate for public office.

4. Notwithstanding any other provision of these Articles, the Corporation shall not carry on any other activities not permitted to be carried on (a) by a Corporation exempt from federal income tax under Section 501(c)(3) of the Internal Revenue Code, (b) by a Corporation, contributions to which are deductible under section 170(c)(2) of the Internal Revenue Code, or (c) by a nonprofit Corporation organized under the laws of the State of _____ pursuant to the provisions of _____ Act.

ARTICLE III

Upon the termination, dissolution or winding up of the Corporation, the Board of Directors shall, after paying or making provision for the payment of all liabilities of the Corporation, distribute all assets of the Corporation to such organization or organizations organized and operated exclusively for charitable, educational or scientific purposes as shall at the time qualify as an exempt organization, or organizations under Section 501(c)(3) of the Internal Revenue Code. Any such assets not so disposed of shall be disposed of by the Court in the County in which the principal office of the Corporation is then located, exclusively for such purposes or to such organization or organizations as said Court shall determine.

Note: In drafting articles of incorporation for a private foundation, an article similar to the following is recommended.

ARTICLE IV

The Corporation shall distribute its income for each tax year at such time and in such manner as not to become subject to the tax on undistributed income imposed by Section 4942 of the Internal Revenue Code. Further, the Corporation shall not engage in any act of self-dealing as defined in Section 4941(d) of the Internal Revenue Code, nor retain any excess business holdings as defined in Section 4943(c) of the Internal Revenue Code, nor make any investments in such manner as to incur tax liability under Section 4944 of the Internal Revenue Code, nor make any taxable expenditures as defined in Section 4945(d) of the Internal Revenue Code.

ARTICLE V

The Corporation shall be organized on a non-stock basis and shall have no members. The authority for all affairs of the Corporation shall be in a Board of Directors who shall have and may exercise all the powers of the Corporation as permitted by federal law, state law, these Articles of Incorporation and the Bylaws of the Corporation as from time to time in effect. The first Board of Directors shall be _____ in number, and their names and addresses are as follows:

Name   Address

Name   Address

Name   Address

[State law will prescribe the specific designation of the Corporation and may require a minimum number of directors].

ARTICLE VI

The name and address of the initial registered agent and registered office are:

Registered Agent_____
          First Name   Middle Name   Last Name

Registered Office_____
          Number, Street

_____
      City   State   Zip Code   County

ARTICLE VII

Any amendments to these Articles of Incorporation shall be made in accordance with the provisions of the laws of the State of _____.

ARTICLE VIII

All general or specific references herein made to the Internal Revenue Code shall be deemed to refer to the Internal Revenue Code of 1986 as now in force or later amended, or the corresponding provision of any future United States Internal Revenue law. Similarly, any general or specific references to the laws of the State of _____ shall be deemed to refer to the laws of the State of _____ as now in force or hereafter amended.

We, the Incorporators, declare that we have examined the foregoing Articles of Incorporation and that the statements contained therein are, to the best of our knowledge and belief, true, correct and complete. Executed this _____ day of _____ 19_____.

Signature and Name **Post Office Address**

1. _____ 1. _____
   Signature   Street

   _____   _____
   Name (please print)   City/State/Zip

2. _____ 2. _____
   Signature   Street

   _____   _____
   Name (please print)   City/State/Zip

3. _____ 3. _____
   Signature   Street

   _____   _____
   Name (please print)   City/Street/Zip

SAMPLE BYLAWS

of

THE _____FOUNDATION

ARTICLE I

BOARD OF DIRECTORS

Section 1: General Powers. The affairs of the Corporation shall be managed by its Board of Directors.

Section 2: Number, Tenure and Qualifications. The number of directors on the board shall be not less than _____ nor more than_____. The number of directors shall be fixed from time to time by the Board of Directors and the number so fixed shall comprise the entire Board of Directors. Directors shall be elected annually at the regular annual meeting of the Board of Directors. If the election of the directors shall not be held at such a meeting, such election shall be held as soon thereafter as is conveniently possible. Each director shall hold office until his/her successor shall have been duly elected and shall have qualified or until his/her death or until he/she shall resign. Directors need not be residents of _____.

Section 3: Vacancies. In the case of any vacancy on the Board of Directors through death, resignation, disqualification or other cause, the remaining Directors by an affirmative vote of a majority thereof, may elect a successor to hold office until the next meeting for the election of directors and until the election and qualification of his/her successor.

Section 4: Removal. A director may be removed for cause by a vote of two thirds (2/3) of all directors then in office. Such action shall be taken at a regular meeting of the Board of Directors or at a special meeting called for such purpose, and the proposed removal shall be set forth in the notice of any such regular or special meeting, sent at least ten (10) days prior thereto.

Section 5: Compensation. Directors shall not receive any stated salaries for their services, but by resolution of the Board of Directors, a fixed sum and expenses of attendance, if any, may be allowed for each regular or special meeting of the Board, providing that nothing herein contained shall be construed to preclude any director from serving the Corporation in any other legally permitted capacity and receiving reasonable compensation therefor.

ARTICLE II
MEETINGS

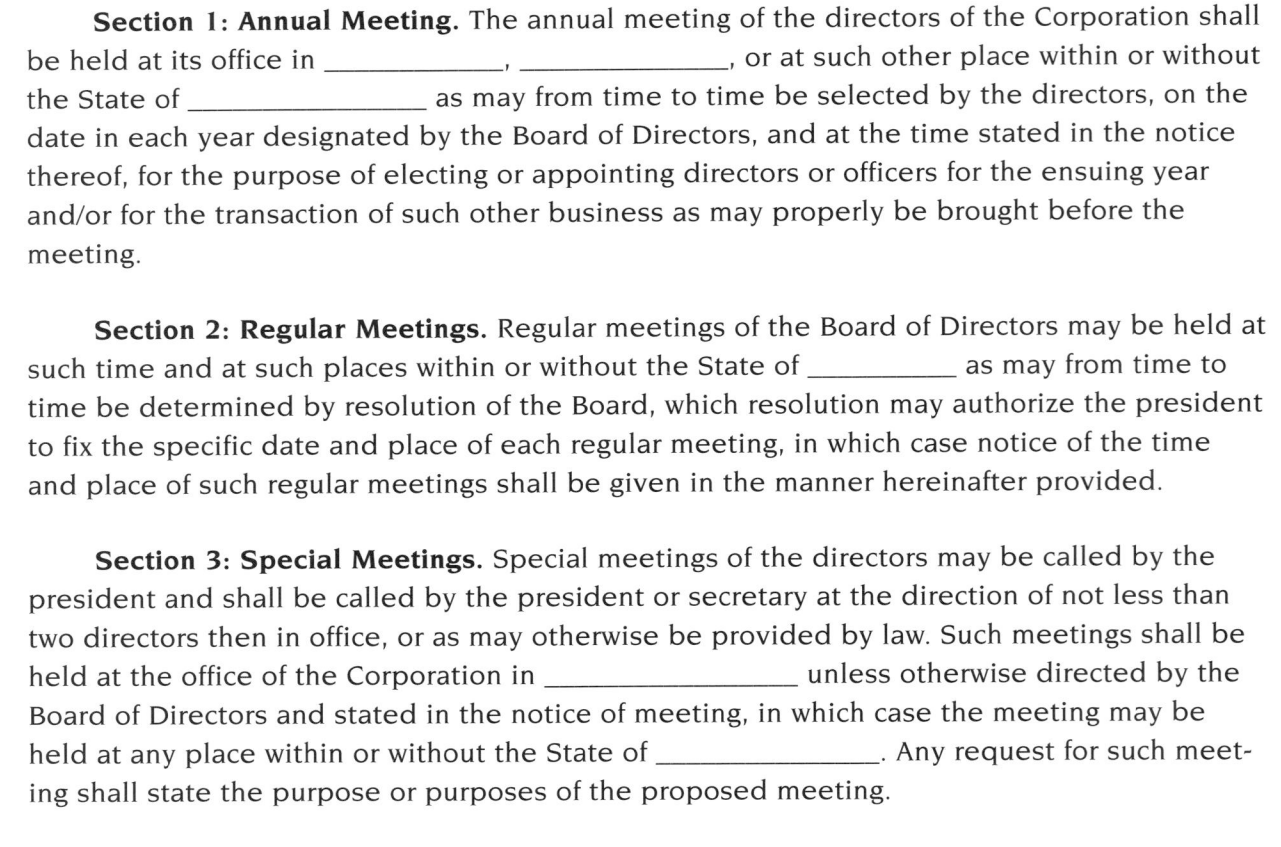

Section 1: Annual Meeting. The annual meeting of the directors of the Corporation shall be held at its office in _____, _____, or at such other place within or without the State of _____ as may from time to time be selected by the directors, on the date in each year designated by the Board of Directors, and at the time stated in the notice thereof, for the purpose of electing or appointing directors or officers for the ensuing year and/or for the transaction of such other business as may properly be brought before the meeting.

Section 2: Regular Meetings. Regular meetings of the Board of Directors may be held at such time and at such places within or without the State of _____ as may from time to time be determined by resolution of the Board, which resolution may authorize the president to fix the specific date and place of each regular meeting, in which case notice of the time and place of such regular meetings shall be given in the manner hereinafter provided.

Section 3: Special Meetings. Special meetings of the directors may be called by the president and shall be called by the president or secretary at the direction of not less than two directors then in office, or as may otherwise be provided by law. Such meetings shall be held at the office of the Corporation in _____ unless otherwise directed by the Board of Directors and stated in the notice of meeting, in which case the meeting may be held at any place within or without the State of _____. Any request for such meeting shall state the purpose or purposes of the proposed meeting.

Section 4: Notice. Notice of the regular annual meeting and any special meeting of the Board of Directors shall be given at least ten (10) days previously thereto by written notice to each director at his or her address as shown by the records of the Corporation. If mailed, such notice shall be deemed to be delivered when deposited in the United States mail in a sealed envelope so addressed with postage thereon prepaid. If notice be given by telegram, such notice shall be deemed to be delivered when the telegram is delivered to the telegraph company. Notice of the annual meeting or any special meeting of the Board of Directors may be waived in writing signed by the person or persons entitled to the notice either before or after the time of the meeting.

The attendance of a director at any meeting shall constitute a waiver of notice of such meeting, except where a director attends a meeting for the express purpose of objecting to the transaction of any business because the meeting is not lawfully called or convened. Neither the business to be transacted at, nor the purpose of, any regular or special meeting of the board need be specified in the notice or waiver of notice of such meeting, unless specifically required by law or by these bylaws.

Section 5: Quorum. A majority of the directors then in office shall constitute a quorum for the transaction of business and the action of a majority of the directors present at a meeting at which a quorum is present shall be the action of the Board of directors except as action by a majority of the directors then in office may be specifically required by statute or other sections of the bylaws.

Section 6: Conduct of Meetings. Meetings of the directors shall be presided over by the president. The secretary or an assistant secretary of the Corporation or, in their absence, a person chosen at the meeting shall act as secretary of the meeting.

Section 7: Action by Unanimous Written Consent. If and when the directors shall severally or collectively consent in writing to any action to be taken by the Corporation either before or after the action is taken, such action shall be as valid a corporate action as though it had been authorized at a meeting of the directors and the written comments shall be filed with the minutes of the proceedings of the Board of Directors.

Section 8: Telephone Conferences. A director may participate in a meeting of directors by a conference telephone or similar communication equipment by which all persons participating in the meeting may hear each other if all participants are advised of the communications equipment and the names of the participants in the conference are divulged to all participants. Participation in a meeting pursuant to this section constitutes presence in person at the meeting.

Section 9: General Powers as to Negotiable Paper. The Board of Directors shall, from time to time, prescribe the manner of signature or endorsement of checks, drafts, notes, acceptances, bills of exchange, obligations, and other negotiable paper or other instruments for the payment of money and designate the officer or officers, agent or agents who shall from time to time be authorized to make, sign or endorse the same on behalf of the Corporation.

Section 10: Powers as to Other Documents. The Board of Directors may authorize any officer or officers, agent or agents, to enter into any contract or execute or deliver any conveyance or other instruments in the name of the Corporation and such authority may be general or confined to specific instances. When the execution of any contract, conveyance or other instrument has been authorized without specification of the officers authorized to execute, the same may be executed on behalf of the Corporation by the president or vice president, by the secretary, an assistant secretary, the treasurer or an assistant treasurer.

ARTICLE III
OFFICERS

Section 1: Officers. The officers of the Corporation shall be a resident, one or more vice presidents, a secretary, a treasurer and such assistant secretaries or other officers as may be elected by the Board of Directors. Officers whose authority and duties are not prescribed in these bylaws shall have the authority to perform the duties prescribed from time to time by the Board of Directors. Any two or more offices may be held by the same person except the offices of president and secretary.

Section 2: Term of Office. The term of office of all officers shall commence upon their election or appointment and shall continue until the next annual meeting of the Corporation and thereafter until their respective successors are chosen or until their resignation or removal. An officer may resign by written notice to the Corporation. The resignation shall be effective upon its receipt by the Corporation or at a subsequent time specified in the notice of resignation. The directors shall have the power to fill any vacancies in any offices occurring for whatever reason.

Section 3: Compensation. The officers of the Corporation shall receive such reasonable compensation for their service as may, from time to time, be fixed by the Board of Directors provided that the compensation of any officer who is also a director shall be fixed by a majority of the Board of Directors then in office.

Section 4: Removal. Any officer elected or appointed by the Board of Directors may be removed by the Board of Directors, whenever in its judgment the best interests of the Corporation would be served thereby, but such removal shall be without prejudice to the contract rights, if any, of the person so removed.

Section 5: President. The president shall be the principal executive officer of the Corporation. Subject to the direction and control of the Board of Directors, he/she shall be in charge of the business and affairs of the Corporation: he/she shall see that the resolutions and directives of the Board of Directors are carried into effect except in those instances in which responsibility is assigned to some other person by the Board of Directors; and in general he/she shall discharge all duties incident to the office of president and such other duties as may be prescribed by the Board of Directors. Except in those instances in which the authority to execute is expressly delegated to another officer or agent of the Corporation or a different mode of execution is expressly prescribed by the Board of Directors, he/she may execute for the Corporation any contracts, deeds, mortgages, bonds or other instruments which the Board of Directors has authorized to be executed either under or without the seal of the Corporation and either individually or with the secretary, and assistant secretary or any other officer thereunto authorized by the Board of Directors, according to the requirements of the form of the instrument. He/she may vote all securities which the Corporation is entitled to vote except as, and to the extent, such authority shall be vested in a different office or agent of the Corporation by the Board of Directors.

Section 6: Vice Presidents. The vice presidents designated by the Board of Directors or, lacking such designation, by the president, shall, in the absence or disability of the president, perform the duties and exercise the powers of the president and shall perform such other duties as the Board of Directors shall prescribe.

Section 7: Secretary. The secretary shall attend all meetings of the Board of Directors and record all votes and the minutes of all proceedings in a book to be kept for that purpose. He/she shall give, or cause to be given, notice of all meetings of the directors for which notice may be required, and shall perform such other duties as may be prescribed by the directors or by the president, under whose supervision, he/she shall act. He/she shall execute with the president all authorized conveyances, contracts or other obligations in the name of the Corporation except as otherwise directed by the directors.

Section 8: Treasurer. The treasurer shall have custody of the funds and securities of the corporation and shall keep full and accurate accounts of receipts and disbursements in books belonging to the Corporation and shall deposit all monies and other valuable effects in the name and to the credit of the Corporation in such depositories as may be designated by the directors. He/she shall disburse the funds of the Corporation as may be ordered by the directors, taking proper vouchers for such disbursements, and shall render to the president and directors, at the regular meetings of the directors, or whenever they may require it, an account of all his/her transactions as treasurer of the Corporation. If required by the directors, he/she shall give the Corporation a bond in such sum and with such surety or sureties as shall be satisfactory to the directors for the faithful performance of the duties of his/her office and for the restoration to the Corporation (in case of his/her death, resignation, or removal from office) of all books, paper, vouchers, money and other property of whatever kind in his/her possession or under his/her control belonging to the Corporation.

Section 9: Assistant Secretaries and Assistant Treasurers. The assistant secretaries and the assistant treasurers respectively (in the order designated by the directors or, lacking such designation, by the president), in the absence of the secretary or treasurer as the case may be, shall perform the duties and exercise the powers of such secretary or treasurer and shall perform such other duties as the directors shall prescribe.

ARTICLE IV
COMMITTEES

Section 1: Committees of Directors. The Board of Directors, by resolution adopted by a majority of the directors, may designate one or more committees, each of which shall consist of two or more directors, which committees, to the extent provided in said resolution and not restricted by law, shall have and exercise the authority and act on behalf of the Board of Directors in the management of the Corporation; but the designation of such committees and the delegation thereto of authority shall not operate to relieve the Board of Directors, or any individual director, of any responsibility imposed upon it or him/her by law.

Section 2: Term of Office. Each member of a committee shall continue as such until his/her successor is appointed, unless the committee shall be sooner terminated, or unless such member be removed from such committee, or unless such member shall cease to qualify as a member thereof.

Section 3: Chair. One member of each committee shall be appointed chair.

Section 4: Vacancies. Vacancies in the membership of any committee may be filled by appointments made in the same manner as provided in the case of the original appointments.

Section 5: Quorum. Unless otherwise provided in the resolution of the Board of Directors designating a committee, a majority of the whole committee shall constitute a quorum and the act of a majority of the members present at a meeting at which a quorum is present shall be the act of the committee.

Section 6: Rules. Each committee may adopt rules for its own governance not inconsistent with these bylaws or with rules adopted by the Board of Directors.

Note: The next article of the bylaws on indemnification and insurance may need to be revised for a corporation that is a private foundation; however, all organizations should consider a similar provision. State laws differ as to what may or may not be indemnified or insured and the bylaws should conform accordingly.

ARTICLE V
INDEMNIFICATION AND INSURANCE

Section 1. The Corporation may indemnify any person who was or is a party, or is threatened to be made a party to any threatened, pending or completed action, suit or proceeding, whether civil, criminal, administrative or investigative (other than an action by or in the right of the Corporation) by reason of the fact that he/she is or was a director, officer, employee or agent of the Corporation, or who is or was serving at the request of the Corporation as a director, officer, employee, or agent of another Corporation, partnership, joint venture, trust or other enterprise, against expenses (including attorney's fees), judgments, fines and amounts paid in settlement actually and reasonably incurred by him/her in connection with such action, suit or proceeding, if he/she acted in good faith and in a manner he/she reasonably believed to be in, or not opposed to the best interests of the Corporation, and, with respect to any criminal action or proceeding, had no reasonable cause to believe his/her conduct was unlawful. The termination of any action, suit or proceeding by judgment, order, settlement, conviction, or upon a plea of nolo contendere or its equivalent, shall not, of itself, create a presumption that the person did not act in good faith and in a manner which he/she reasonably believed to be in or not opposed to the best interests of the Corporation, and, with respect to any criminal action or proceeding, had reasonable cause to believe that his/her conduct was unlawful.

Section 2. The Corporation may indemnify any person who was or is a party, or is threatened to be made a party to any threatened, pending or completed action or suit by or in the right of the Corporation to procure a judgment in its favor by reason of the fact that he/she is or was a director, officer, employee or agent of the Corporation, or is or was serving at the request of the Corporation as a director, officer, employee or agent of another Corporation, partnership, joint venture, trust or other enterprise, against expenses (including attorney's fees) actually and reasonably incurred by him/her in connection with the defense or settlement of such action or suit, if he/she acted in good faith and in a manner he/she reasonably believed to be in, or not opposed to the best interests of the Corporation, and except that no indemnification shall be made in respect of any claim, issue or matter as to which such person shall have been adjudged to be liable for negligence or misconduct in the performance of his/her duty to the Corporation, unless, and only to the extent that the court in which such action or suit was brought shall determine upon application that, despite the adjudication of liability, but in view of all the circumstances of the case, such person is fairly and reasonably entitled to indemnity for such expenses as the court shall deem proper.

Section 3. To the extent that a director, officer, employee or agent of the Corporation has been successful, on the merits or otherwise, in the defense of any action, suit or proceeding referred to in Sections (1) and (2) of this Article V, or in defense of any claim, issue or matter therein, he/she shall be indemnified against expenses (including attorneys" fees) actually and reasonably incurred by him/her in connection therewith.

Section 4. Any indemnification under Section (1) and (2) of this Article V (unless ordered by a court) shall be made by the Corporation only as authorized in the specific case, upon a determination that indemnification of the director, officer, employee or agent is proper in the circumstances because he/she has met the applicable standard of conduct set forth in Sections (1) and (2) of this Article V. Such determination shall be made (i) by the Board of Directors by a majority vote of a quorum consisting of directors who were not parties to such action, suit or proceeding, or (ii) if such a quorum is not obtainable, or, even if obtainable, a quorum of disinterested directors so directs, by independent legal counsel in a written opinion.

Section 5. Expenses incurred in defending a civil or criminal action, suit or proceeding may be paid by the Corporation in advance of the final disposition of such action, suit or proceeding, as authorized by the Board of Directors in the specific case, upon receipt of an undertaking by or on behalf of the director, officer, employee or agent to repay such amount, unless it shall ultimately be determined that he/she is entitled to be indemnified by the Corporation as authorized in this Article V.

Section 6. The indemnification provided by this Article V shall not be deemed exclusive of any other rights to which those seeking indemnification may be entitled under any agreement, vote of disinterested directors, or otherwise, both as to action in his/her official capacity and as to action in another capacity while holding such office, and shall continue as to a person who has ceased to be a director, officer, employee or agent, and shall inure to the benefit of the heirs, executors and administrators of such a person.

Section 7. The Corporation may purchase and maintain insurance on behalf of any person who is or was a director, officer, employee or agent of the Corporation, or who is or was serving at the request of the Corporation as a direct, officer, employee, or agent of another corporation, partnership, joint venture, trust or other enterprise, against any liability asserted against him/her and incurred by him/her in any such capacity, or arising out of his/her status as such, whether or not the Corporation would have the power to indemnify him/her against such liability under the provisions of the Article V.

ARTICLE VI
BOOKS AND RECORDS

The Corporation shall keep correct and complete books and records of account and shall also keep minutes of the proceedings of its Board of Directors and committees having any of the authority of the Board of Directors.

ARTICLE VII
FISCAL YEAR

The fiscal year of the Corporation shall be fixed by resolution of the Board of Directors

ARTICLE VIII
SEAL

The corporate seal shall have inscribed thereon the name of the Corporation and the words "Corporate Seal,_____."

ARTICLE IX
WAIVER OF NOTICE

Whenever any notice is required to be given under the provision of the Act of the State of _____ or under the provisions of the Articles of Incorporation or the bylaws of the Corporation, a waiver thereof in writing signed by the person or person entitled by such notice, whether before or after the time stated therein, shall be deemed equivalent to the giving of such notice.

ARTICLE X
AMENDMENTS

The power to alter, amend or repeal the bylaws or adopt new bylaws shall be vested in the Board of Directors. Such action may be taken at a regular or special meeting for which written notices of the purpose shall be given. The bylaws may contain any provisions for the regulation and management of the affairs of the Corporation not inconsistent with law or the Articles of Incorporation.

SAMPLE TRUST AGREEMENT*

> NOTE: The trust agreement here provided is designed for forming a private foundation and is not a model to copy; rather it is provided purely to illustrate what such a document might look like. Each state will have its own form or particular requirements to follow, and they may differ widely from state to state.

THIS AGREEMENT, creating the _____ Foundation, is made at _____, _____, this day of _____, 19___, between _____, _____, _____, as the Settlor and _____, as the Trustees.

The Settlor hereby transfers the property listed on Schedule A attached hereto to the Trustees, and the Trustees hereby acknowledge receipt thereof and agree to hold such property and all investments and reinvestments thereof irrevocably in trust as the "trust estate," upon the following terms and conditions:

ARTICLE I

The name of this Trust shall be the _____ Foundation.

ARTICLE II

The Trust is created exclusively for charitable, religious, scientific, literary or educational purposes, including, for such purposes, the making of distributions to organizations that qualify as exempt organizations under Section 501(c)(3) of the Internal Revenue Code of 1986 (or the corresponding provision of any future United States Internal Revenue law).

ARTICLE III

The Trustees may receive and accept property, whether real, personal or mixed, by way of gift, bequest or devise, from any person, firm, trust or corporation, to be held, administered and disposed of in accordance with and pursuant to the provisions of this Trust Agreement; but no gift, bequest or devise of any such property shall be received and accepted if it is conditioned or limited in such manner (a) as to require the disposition of the income or its principal to any person or organization other than a charitable organization or for other than "charitable purposes" within the meaning of such terms as defined in paragraphs (h) and (i) of Article VI of this Trust Agreement, or (b) as shall in the opinion of the Trustees, jeopardize the

---

*With minor changes, the Sample Trust Agreement here is based on and reprinted with permission from A *Lawyer's Guide to Private Foundations*, by Susan N. Garry, copyright 1985 by Mayer, Brown & Platt, a publication of the Donors Forum of Chicago.

federal income tax exemption of this Trust pursuant to Section 501 (c)(3) of the Internal Revenue Code of 1986 (or the corresponding provision of any future United States Internal Revenue law).

ARTICLE IV

(a) The principal and income of all property received and accepted by the Trustees to be administered under this Trust Agreement shall be held in trust by them, and the Trustees may make payments or distributions from income or principal, or both, to or for the benefit of such one or more organizations that qualify as exempt organizations under Section 501 (c)(3) of the Internal Revenue Code of 1986 (or the corresponding provision of any future United States Internal Revenue law), as the Trustees shall from time to time determine; and the Trustees may make payments or distributions from income or principal, or both, directly for the charitable purposes of this Trust, as defined in paragraph (i) of Article VI, as the Trustees shall from time to time determine.

(b) No part of the net earnings of this Trust shall inure or be payable to or for the benefit of any private individual, and no part of the activities of this Trust shall be the carrying on of propaganda, or otherwise attempting to influence legislation as defined in Section 4945(e) of the Internal Revenue Code of 1986 (or the corresponding provision of any future United States Internal Revenue law).

(c) No part of the activities of this Trust shall be the participation in, or intervention in (including the publishing or distributing of statements), any political campaign on behalf of any candidate for public office.

(d) The Trustees shall distribute the income of this Trust for each tax year at such time and in such manner as not to become subject to the tax on undistributed income imposed by Section 4942 of the Internal Revenue Code of 1986 (or the corresponding provision of any future United States Internal Revenue law). Further, the Trustees shall not engage in any act of self-dealing as defined in Section 4941 (d) of the Internal Revenue Code of 1986 (or the corresponding provision of any future United States Internal Revenue law), nor retain any excess business holding as defined in Section 4943(c) of the Internal Revenue Code of 1986 (or the corresponding provision of any future United States Internal Revenue law), nor make any investments in such manner as to incur tax liability under Section 4944 of the Internal Revenue Code of 1986 (or the corresponding provision of any future United States Internal Revenue law), nor make any taxable expenditures as defined in Section 4945(d) of the Internal Revenue Code of 1986 (or the corresponding provision of any future United States Internal Revenue law).

ARTICLE V

This Trust Agreement may be amended at any time or times by written instrument or instruments signed and acknowledged by the Trustees, provided that no amendment shall authorize the Trustees to conduct the affairs of this Trust in any manner or for any purpose contrary to the provisions of Section 501 (c)(3) of the Internal Revenue Code of 1986 (or the corresponding provision of any future United States Internal Revenue law). An amendment of the provisions of this Article V (or any amendment to it) shall be valid only if and to the extent that such amendment further restricts the Trustees' amending power. All instruments amending this Declaration of Trust shall be noted upon or kept attached to the executed original of this Trust Agreement held by the Trustees.

ARTICLE VI

(a) Any Trustee under this Trust Agreement may, by written instrument, signed and acknowledged, resign his or her office. The number of Trustees shall be at all times not less than _____, and whenever for any reason the number is reduced below _____, there shall be, and at any other time there may be, appointed one or more additional Trustees. Appointments shall be made by the Trustee or Trustees for the time in office by written instruments signed and acknowledged.

(b) Upon any change in any trusteeship hereunder, the continuing Trustee or the next successor Trustee or Trustees, as the case may be, shall have all of the powers, authorities, rights, discretion, immunities, estates, titles, duties and obligations of the original Trustees, without the necessity of any conveyance or the taking of any action whatsoever.

(c) None of the Trustees shall be required to furnish any bond or surety. None of them shall be responsible or liable for the acts or omissions of any other of the Trustees or of any predecessor or of a custodian, agent, depositary or counsel selected with reasonable care.

(d) The Trustee or Trustees from time to time in office, shall have full authority to act even though one or more vacancies may exist. A Trustee may, by appropriate written instrument, delegate all or any part of his/her powers to another or others of the Trustees for such periods and subject to such conditions as such delegating Trustee may determine.

(e) The Trustees serving under this Trust Agreement are authorized to pay to themselves amounts for reasonable expenses incurred and reasonable compensation for personal services rendered in the administration of this Trust.

(f) The Trust shall continue forever unless the Trustees terminate it and distribute all of the principal and income, which action may be taken by the Trustees in their discretion at any time; provided, however, that if and to the extent that state law prohibits perpetual duration, this Trust shall not extend beyond the maximum period permitted under applicable state law. On termination, the trust fund as then constituted shall be distributed to or for the use of such charitable organizations in such amounts and for such charitable purposes as the Trustees shall then select and determine.

(g) The Trustees are authorized to form and organize a not-for-profit corporation limited to the uses and purposes provided for in this Trust Agreement, such corporation to be organized under the laws of any state or under the laws of the United States as may be determined by the Trustees. Such corporation when organized shall have power to administer and control the affairs and property and to carry out the uses, objects, and purposes of this Trust. Upon the creation and organization of such corporation, the Trustees are authorized and empowered to convey, transfer and deliver to such corporation all the property and assets to which this Trust may be or become entitled. The articles, bylaws and other provisions for the organization and management of such corporation and its affairs and property shall be such as the Trustees shall determine, consistent with the provisions of this paragraph.

(h) In this Trust Agreement and in any amendments to it, references to charitable organizations" or "charitable organization" mean corporations, trusts, funds, foundations or community chests created or organized in the United States or in any of its possessions, whether under the laws of the United States, any state or territory, the District of Columbia or any possession of the United States, organized and operated exclusively for charitable purposes, no part of the net earnings of which inures or is payable to or for the benefit of any private shareholder or individual, and no part of the activities of which is carrying on propaganda, or otherwise attempting to influence legislation, and which do not participate in or intervene in (including the publishing or distributing of statements), any political campaign on behalf of any candidate for public office. It is intended that the organization described in this paragraph (h) shall be entitled to exemption from federal income tax under Section 501 (c)(3) of the Internal Revenue Code of 1986 (or the corresponding provisions of any future United States Internal Revenue law).

(i) In this Trust Agreement and in any amendments to it, the term "charitable purposes" shall be limited to and shall include only charitable, religious, scientific, literary or educational purposes within the meaning of those terms as used in Section 501 (c)(3) of the Internal Revenue Code of 1986 (or the corresponding provision of any future United States Revenue law), but only such purposes as also constitute charitable purposes under the law of trusts of the State of _____,

ARTICLE VII

The Trustees shall have, in addition to all powers granted by law, and subject to paragraph (e) of Article IV hereof, the following powers with respect to this Trust, exercisable in the Trustees' discretion:

(a) To invest and reinvest the principal and income of the Trust in such property, real, personal or mixed, and in such manner as they shall deem proper, and from time to time change investments as they shall deem advisable; to invest in or retain any stocks, shares, bonds, notes, obligations, or personal or real property (including without limitation any interests in or obligations of any corporation, partnership, association, business trust, investment trust, common trust fund or investment company) although some or all of the property so acquired or retained is of a kind or size which but for this express authority would not be considered proper and although all of the trust funds are invested in the securities of one company. No principal or income, however, shall be loaned, directly or indirectly, to any Trustee or to anyone else, corporate or otherwise, who has at any time made a contribution to this Trust, nor to anyone except on the basis of an adequate interest charge and with adequate security.

(b) To sell, lease or exchange any personal, mixed or real property, at public auction or by private contract, for such consideration and on such terms as to credit or otherwise, and to make such contracts and enter into such undertakings relating to the trust property, as the Trustees consider advisable, whether or not such leases or contracts may extend beyond the duration of this Trust.

(c) To borrow money for such periods, at such rates of interest, and upon such terms as the Trustees consider advisable, and as security for such loans to mortgage or pledge any real or personal property with or without power of sale; to acquire or hold any real or personal property, subject to any mortgage or pledge on or of property acquired or held by this Trust.

(d) To execute and deliver deeds, assignments, transfers, mortgages, pledges, leases, covenants, contracts, promissory notes, releases and other instruments, sealed or unsealed, incident to any transaction in which the Trustees engage.

(e) To vote, to give proxies, to participate in the reorganization, merger or consolidation of any concern, or in the sale, lease, disposition or distribution of its assets; to join with other security holders in acting through a committee, depositary, voting trustees, or otherwise, and in this connection to delegate authority to such committee, depositary, or trustees and to deposit securities with them or transfer securities to them, to pay assessments levied on securities or to exercise subscription rights in respect of securities.

(f) To employ a bank or trust company as custodian of any funds or securities and to delegate to it such powers as the Trustees deem appropriate; to hold trust property without indication of fiduciary capacity but only in the name of a registered nominee, provided the trust property is at all times identified as such on the books of this Trust; to keep any or all of the trust property or funds in any place or places in the United States of America; to employ clerks, accountants, investment counsel, agents, attorneys and any special services, and to pay the reasonable compensation and expenses of all such services in addition to the compensation of the Trustees.

ARTICLE VIII

The Trustees' powers are exercisable solely in the fiduciary capacity consistent with and in furtherance of the charitable purposes of this Trust as specified in paragraph (i) of Article VI and not otherwise.

ARTICLE IX

The term "Trustees" as used in this instrument shall include the original Trustees and any successor or continuing Trustee or Trustees at the time acting. Where appropriate, with reference to the Trustees, the use of the masculine shall include the feminine and the neuter, and the plural shall include the singular, and vice versa.

ARTICLE X

Any person may rely on a copy, certified by a notary public, of the executed original of this Trust Agreement held by the Trustees, and of any of the notations on it and writings attached to it, as fully as he might rely on the original documents themselves. Any such person may rely fully on any statements of fact certified by anyone who appears from such original documents or from such certified copy to be a Trustee under this Trust Agreement. No one dealing with the Trustees need inquire concerning the validity of anything the Trustees purport to do. No one dealing with the Trustees need see to the application of anything paid or transferred to or upon the order of the Trustees of this Trust.

ARTICLE XI

The validity, effect and construction of this Trust shall be determined in accordance with the laws of _____. The original situs and original place of administration of the trust estate shall also be _____, but the situs and place of administration of the trust estate may, however, be transferred at any time or from time to time to such place or places as the Trustees deem to be for the best interest of the trust estate. In so doing, the Trustees may resign and appoint a substitute Trustee, but may remove each substitute Trustee and appoint another, including any one or more of the appointing Trustees, at will. Each substitute Trustee so appointed may delegate any and all of such substitute Trustee's powers, discretionary or ministerial, to the appointing Trustees.

IN WITNESS WHEREOF, the Settlor and the original Trustees have executed this Trust Agreement on the day and year first above written.

_____   _____
Settlor   Trustee

                                     _____
                                       Trustee

- -

SCHEDULE A

TO

THE _____ FOUNDATION

TRUST AGREEMENT

Identified:

_____   _____
Settlor   Trustee

                                     _____
                                       Trustee

COUNCIL ON FOUNDATIONS
Principles and Practices for Effective Grantmaking

1. Whatever the nature of the entity engaged in private grantmaking, and whatever its interests, it should seek to establish a set of basic policies that define the program interest and the fundamental objectives to be served.

2. An identifiable board, committee, or other decisionmaking body should have clear responsibility for determining those policies and procedures, causing them to be implemented and reviewing and revising them from time to time.

3. The processes for receiving, examining and deciding on grant applications should be established on a clear and logical basis and should be followed in a manner consistent with the organization's policies and purposes.

4. Responsive grantmakers recognize that accountability extends beyond the narrow requirements of the law. Grantmakers should establish and carry out policies that recognize these multiple obligations for accountability: to the charter provisions by which their founders defined certain basic expectations, to those charitable institutions they serve, to the general public, to the Internal Revenue Service, and to certain state governmental agencies.

5. Open communications with the public and with grantseekers about the policies and procedures that are followed in grantmaking is in the interest of all concerned and is important if the grantmaking process is to function well, and if trust in the responsibility and accountability of grantmakers is to be maintained.

    A brief written statement about policies, program interests, grantmaking practices, geographic and policy restrictions and preferred ways of receiving applications is recommended. Prompt acknowledgment of the receipt of any serious application is important. Grantseekers whose programs and proposals fall outside the interests of the grantmakers should be told this immediately and those whose proposals are still under consideration should be informed, insofar as is possible, of the steps and timing that will be taken in reaching the final decision.

6. Beyond the filing of forms required by government, grantmakers should consider possible ways of informing the public concerning their stewardship through publication and distribution of periodic reports, preferably annual reports, possibly supplemented by newsletters, reports to The Foundation Center, and the use of other communications channels.

7. The preservation and enhancement of an essential community of interest between the grantor and grantee requires that their relationship be based on mutual respect, candor and understanding with each investing the necessary time and attention to define clearly the purposes of the grant, the expectations as to reports related to financial and other matters and the provisions for evaluating and publicizing projects.

    Many grantmakers, going beyond the providing of money, help grantees through such other means as assisting in the sharpening of the objectives, monitoring the performance, evaluating the outcome and encouraging early planning for future stages.

8. It is important that grantmakers be alert and responsive to changing conditions in society and to the changing needs and merits of particular grantseeking organizations. Responses to needs and social conditions may well be determined by independent inquiries, not merely by reactions to requests submitted by grantseekers. In responding to new challenges, grantmakers are helped if they use the special knowledge, experience and insight of individuals beyond those persons, families or corporations from which the funds originally came. Some grantmakers find it useful to secure ideas and comments from a variety of consultants and advisory panels, as well as diversified staff and board members. In view of the historic under representation of minorities and women in supervisory and policy positions, particular attention should be given to finding ways to draw them into the decision-making processes.

9. From time to time, all grantmaking organizations should review their program interests, basic policies, board and staff composition, and assess the overall results of their grantmaking.

10. Beyond the legal requirements that forbid staff, board members and their families from profiting financially from any philanthropic grant, it is important that grantmakers weigh carefully all circumstances in which there exists the possibility of accusations of self-interest. In particular, staff and board members should disclose to the governing body the nature of their personal or family affiliation or involvement with any organizations for which a grant is considered, even though such affiliation may not give rise to any pecuniary conflict of interest.

11. Grantmakers should maintain interaction with others in the field of philanthropy including such bodies as regional associations of grantmakers, The Foundation Center, the Council on Foundations and various local, regional, and national independent sector organizations. They should bear in mind that they share with others responsibility for strengthening the effectiveness of the many private initiatives to serve the needs and interests of the public and for enhancing general understanding and support of such private initiatives within the community and the nation.

—Approved by the Board of Directors on June 16, 1980.

—On November 4, 1982, the Board required that all members subscribe to the above statement.

FORM 1023

On the following pages, the reader will find reproduced actual pages from the Form 1023 and its instructions (as last revised by the Internal Revenue Service in April 1996). This form is used to apply for tax exempt status at the federal level. This form is regularly revised and updated by the IRS. You can obtain the most current version by calling 1-800-424-3676.

Note: Not all pages from Form 1023 are provided here; we have only included those pages and instructions relevant for formation of a grantmaking foundation. Those parts of the form relating to churches, hospitals, universities, homes for the aged, day care centers, etc., have not been included.

**Department of the Treasury
Internal Revenue Service**

Application for Recognition of Exemption

Under Section 501(c)(3) of the Internal Revenue Code

Contents:
Form 1023 and
  Instructions
Form 872-C

Note: *For the addresses for filing* **Form 1023,** *see* **Form 8718,** *User Fee for Exempt Organization Letter Request. For obtaining an employer identification number (EIN), see* **Form SS-4,** *Application for Employer Identification Number.*

**Package 1023
(Rev. April 1996)**

Cat. No. 47194L

Department of the Treasury
Internal Revenue Service

Instructions for Form 1023

(Revised April 1996)

Application for Recognition of Exemption Under Section 501(c)(3) of the Internal Revenue Code

Section references are to the Internal Revenue Code unless otherwise noted.

Note: *Retain a copy of the completed Form 1023 in the organization's permanent records. See* **Public Inspection of Form 1023** *regarding public inspection of approved applications.*

Paperwork Reduction Act Notice.—We ask for the information on this form to carry out the Internal Revenue laws of the United States. If you want your organization to be recognized as tax-exempt by the IRS, you are required to give us this information. We need it to determine whether the organization meets the legal requirements for tax-exempt status.

The organization is not required to provide the information requested on a form that is subject to the Paperwork Reduction Act unless the form displays a valid OMB control number. Books or records relating to a form or its instructions must be retained as long as their contents may become material in the administration of any Internal Revenue law. The rules governing the confidentiality of the Form 1023 application are covered in Code section 6104.

The time needed to complete and file these forms will vary depending on individual circumstances. The estimated average times are:

Form	Recordkeeping	Learning about the law or the form	Preparing, and sending the form to IRS
1023 Parts I to IV	55 hr., 29 min.	4 hr., 37 min.	8 hr., 7 min.
1023 Sch. A	7 hr., 10 min.	-0- min.	7 min.
1023 Sch. B	4 hr., 47 min.	30 min.	36 min.
1023 Sch. C	5 hr., 1 min.	35 min.	43 min.
1023 Sch. D	4 hr., 4 min.	42 min.	47 min.
1023 Sch. E	9 hr., 20 min.	1 hr., 5 min.	1 hr., 17 min.
1023 Sch. F	2 hr., 39 min.	2 hr., 53 min.	3 hr., 3 min.
1023 Sch. G	2 hr., 38 min.	-0- min.	2 min.
1023 Sch. H	1 hr., 55 min.	42 min.	46 min.
1023 Sch. I	3 hr., 35 min.	-0- min.	4 min.
872-C	1 hr., 26 min.	24 min.	26 min.

If you have comments concerning the accuracy of these time estimates or suggestions for making these forms simpler, we would be happy to hear from you. You can write to the Tax Forms Committee, Western Area Distribution Center, Rancho Cordova, CA 95743-0001. **DO NOT** send the application to this address. Instead, see **Where To File** on page 2.

General Instructions

User fee.—A user fee must be paid with determination letter requests submitted to the Internal Revenue Service. **Form 8718,** User Fee for Exempt Organization Determination Letter Request, must be submitted with this application along with the appropriate fee as stated on Form 8718. Form 8718 may be obtained through your local IRS office or by calling the telephone number given below for obtaining forms and publications.

Helpful information.—For additional information, get **Pub. 557,** Tax-Exempt Status for Your Organization; **Pub. 578,** Tax Information for Private Foundations and Foundation Managers; and **Pub. 598,** Tax on Unrelated Business Income of Exempt Organizations. You may also call 1-800-829-4477 to listen to recorded tax information. A touch-tone telephone is required. **Topic #310,** Tax-exempt status for organizations, and **Topic #311,** How to apply for exempt status, are informative. These topic numbers may change. If so, listen to the directory of topics for the new topic numbers or refer to the instructions for a current **Form 1040,** U.S. Individual Income Tax Return, for the updated list of Tele-Tax Topics. For additional forms and publications, call 1-800-829-3676 (1-800-**Tax-Form**).

Purpose of Form

1. Completed Form 1023 required for section 501(c)(3) exemption.—Unless it meets either of the exceptions in item 2 below, or notifies the IRS that it is applying for recognition of section 501(c)(3) exempt status, no organization formed after October 9, 1969, will be considered tax-exempt under section 501(c)(3).

An organization notifies the IRS by filing a completed Form 1023. Form 1023 also solicits the information that the IRS needs to determine if the organization is a private foundation.

2. Organizations not required to file Form 1023.—The following organizations will be considered tax-exempt under section 501(c)(3) even if they do not file Form 1023: **(a)** churches, their integrated auxiliaries, and conventions or associations of churches, or **(b)** any organization that is not a private foundation (as defined in section 509(a)) and that has gross receipts in each taxable year of normally not more than $5,000.

Even if these organizations are not required to file Form 1023 to be tax-exempt, they may wish to file Form 1023 and receive a determination letter of IRS recognition of their section 501(c)(3) status to obtain certain incidental benefits such as public recognition of their tax-exempt status; exemption from certain state taxes; advance assurance to donors of deductibility of contributions; exemption from certain Federal excise taxes; nonprofit mailing privileges, etc.

3. Other organizations.—In applying for a determination letter, cooperative service organizations, described in section 501(e) and (f), and child care organizations, described in section 501(k), use Form 1023 and are treated as section 501(c)(3) organizations.

4. Group exemption letter.—Generally, Form 1023 is not used to apply for a group exemption letter. For information on how to apply for a group exemption letter, see Pub. 557.

What To File

All applicants must complete pages 1 through 9 of Form 1023. The following organizations must also complete the schedules or form indicated:

 1. Churches — Schedule A
 2. Schools — Schedule B
 3. Hospitals and Medical Research — Schedule C
 4. Supporting Organizations (509(a)(3)) — Schedule D
 5. Private Operating Foundations — Schedule E
 6. Homes for the Aged or Handicapped — Schedule F
 7. Child Care — Schedule G
 8. Scholarship Benefits or Student Aid — Schedule H
 9. Organizations that have taken over or will take over a "for profit" institution — Schedule I
 10. Organizations requesting an advance ruling in Part III, Line 11 — Form 872-C

Attachments.—State on each attachment that it relates to Form 1023 and identify the applicable part and line item number. Also show on each attachment the organization's name, address, and employer identification number (EIN). Use 8½ by 11 inch paper for attachments.

In addition to the required documents and statements, include with the application any additional information citing court decisions, rulings, opinions, etc., that will expedite processing of the application. Generally, attachments in the form of tape recordings are not acceptable unless accompanied by a transcript.

When To File

An organization formed after October 9, 1969, must file Form 1023 to be recognized as an organization described in section 501(c)(3). Generally, if an organization files its application within 15 months after the end of the month in which it was formed, and if the IRS approves the application, the effective date of the organization's section 501(c)(3) status will be the date it was organized.

Generally, if an organization does not file its application (Form 1023) within 15 months after the end of the month in which it was formed, it will not qualify for exempt status during the period before the date of its application. For exceptions and special rules, including automatic extensions in some cases, see Part III of Form 1023.

Where To File
File the completed application, and all information required, with the IRS key district office for the organization's principal place of business or office as listed in Form 8718. As soon as possible after the complete application is received, you will be advised of the IRS's determination and of the annual returns (if any) that the organization will be required to file.

Signature Requirements
An officer, a trustee who is authorized to sign, or another person authorized by a power of attorney must sign this application. Send the power of attorney with the application when you file it. **Form 2848,** Power of Attorney and Declaration of Representative, may be used for this purpose.

Deductibility of Contributions
Deductions for charitable contributions are not allowed for any gifts or bequests made to organizations that do not qualify under section 501(c)(3). The effective date of an organization's section 501(c)(3) status determines the date that contributions to it are deductible by donors. (See **When To File** on page 1.)

Contributions by U.S. residents to foreign organizations generally are not deductible. Tax treaties between the U.S. and certain foreign countries provide limited exceptions. Foreign organizations (other than those in Canada or Mexico) claiming eligibility to receive contributions deductible by U.S. residents must attach an English copy of the U.S. tax treaty that provides for such deductibility.

Public Inspection of Form 1023
IRS responsibilities.—If the application is approved, it and any supporting documents will be open to public inspection in any key district office and in the Internal Revenue Service's National Office, as required by section 6104. In addition, any letter or other document issued by the IRS with regard to the application will be open to public inspection. However, information relating to a trade secret, patent, style of work, or apparatus that, if released, would adversely affect the organization, or any other information that would adversely affect the national defense, will not be made available for public inspection. Applicants must identify this information by clearly marking it "NOT SUBJECT TO PUBLIC INSPECTION" and attach a statement explaining why the organization asks that the information be withheld. If the IRS agrees, the information will be withheld.

Organization's responsibilities.—The organization must make available for public inspection a copy of its approved application and supporting documents, along with any document or letter issued by the IRS. These must be available during regular business hours at the organization's principal office and at each of its regional or district offices having at least three paid employees. See Notice 88-120, 1988-2 C.B. 454. If any person under a duty to comply with the inspection provisions fails to comply with these requirements, a penalty of $10 a day will be imposed for each day the failure continues.

Appeal Procedures
The organization's application will be considered by the key district office which will either:

1. Issue a favorable determination letter;

2. Issue a proposed adverse determination letter denying the exempt status requested; or

3. Refer the case to the National Office.

If we send you a proposed adverse determination, we will advise you of your appeal rights at that time.

Language and Currency Requirements
Form 1023 and attachments must be prepared in English. If the organizational document or bylaws are in any other language, an English translation must be furnished. If the organization produces or distributes foreign language publications that are submitted with the application, you may be asked to provide English translations for one or more of them during the processing of the application.

Report all financial information in U.S. dollars (specify the conversion rate used). Combine amounts from within and outside the United States and report the total for each item on the financial statements.

For example:

Gross Investment Income

From U.S. sources	$4,000
From non-U.S. sources	1,000
Amount to report on income statement	$5,000

Annual Information Return
If the annual information return for tax-exempt organizations becomes due while its application for recognition of exempt status is pending with the IRS (including any appeal of a proposed adverse determination), the organization should file **Form 990,** Return of Organization Exempt From Income Tax, (or **Form 990-EZ,** Short Form Return of Organization Exempt From Income Tax) and if required, **Schedule A (Form 990),** Organization Exempt Under Section 501(c)(3), or **Form 990-PF,** Return of Private Foundation, if a private foundation, and indicate that an application is pending.

Special Rule for Canadian Colleges and Universities
A Canadian college or university that has received a **Form T2051,** Notification of Registration, from Revenue Canada (Department of National Revenue, Taxation) and whose registration has not been revoked, does not have to complete all parts of Form 1023 that would otherwise be applicable. Such an organization must complete only Part I of Form 1023 and Schedule B (Schools, Colleges, and Universities). The organization must also attach a copy of its **Form T2050,** Application for Registration, together with all the required attachments that it submitted to Revenue Canada. If any attachments were prepared in French, an English translation must be furnished.

Other Canadian organizations seeking a determination of section 501(c)(3) status must complete Form 1023 in the same manner as U.S. organizations.

Specific Instructions
The following instructions are keyed to the line items on the application form:

Part I. Identification of Applicant
Line 1. Full name and address of organization.—Enter the organization's name exactly as it appears in its creating document including amendments. If the organization will be operating under another name, show the other name in parentheses. Enter your nine-digit ZIP code.

If the organization's address is outside the United States or its possessions or territories, enter the information on the line for "City or town, state, and ZIP code" in the following order: city, province or state, foreign postal code, and the name of the foreign country. **Do not** abbreviate the country name.

Line 2. Employer identification number (EIN).—All organizations must have an EIN. Enter the nine-digit EIN assigned to the organization by the IRS. If the organization does **not** have an EIN, get **Form SS-4,** Application for Employer Identification Number, for details on how to obtain an EIN immediately by telephone. If the organization has previously applied for a number, enter "applied for" and attach a statement giving the date of the application and the office where it was filed. **Do not** apply for an EIN more than once.

Line 3. Person to contact.—Enter the name and telephone number of the person to contact during business hours if more information is needed. The contact person should be an officer, director, or a person with power of attorney who is familiar with the organization's activities and is authorized to act on its behalf. Attach Form 2848 or other power of attorney.

Line 4. Month the annual accounting period ends.—Enter the month the organization's annual accounting period ends. The accounting period is usually the 12-month period that is the organization's tax year. The organization's first tax year depends on the accounting period chosen. (The first tax year could be less than 12 months).

Line 5. Date formed.—Enter the date the organization became a legal entity. For a corporation, this is the date that the articles of incorporation were approved by the appropriate state official. For an unincorporated organization, it is the date its constitution or articles of association were adopted.

Line 6. Activity codes.—Select up to three of the code numbers listed on the back cover that best describe or most accurately identify the organization's purposes, activities, or type of organization. Enter the codes in the order of importance.

Line 7.—Indicate if the organization is one of the following:
- 501(e) Cooperative hospital service organization;
- 501(f) Cooperative service organization of operating educational organization;
- 501(k) Organization providing child care.

If none of the above applies, make no entry on line 7.

Line 8.—Indicate if the organization has ever filed a Form 1023 or **Form 1024,** Application for Recognition of Exemption Under Section 501(a), with the IRS.

Line 9.—If the organization for which this application is being filed is a private foundation, answer "N/A." If the organization is not required to file Form 990 (or Form 990-EZ) and is not a private foundation, answer "No" and attach an explanation. Get the Form 990 Instructions and refer to page 2 for a discussion of organizations not required to file Form 990 (or Form 990-EZ). Otherwise, answer "Yes."

Line 10.—Indicate if the organization has ever filed Federal income tax returns as a taxable organization or filed returns as an exempt organization (e.g., Form 990, 990-EZ, 990-PF, or 990-T, Exempt Organization Business Income Tax Return).

Line 11. Type of organization and organizational documents.—Submit a conformed copy of the organizing instrument. If the organization does not have an organizing instrument, it will not qualify for exempt status. A conformed copy is one that agrees with the original and all amendments to it. The conformed copy may be a photocopy of the original signed and dated organizing document OR it may be a copy of the organizing document that is not signed but is accompanied by a written declaration signed by an authorized individual stating that the copy is a complete and accurate copy of the original signed and dated document.

In the case of a corporation, a copy of the articles of incorporation, approved and dated by an appropriate state official, is sufficient by itself. If an unsigned copy of the articles of incorporation is submitted, it must be accompanied by the written declaration discussed above. Signed or unsigned copies of the articles of incorporation must be accompanied by a declaration stating that the original copy of the articles was filed with, and approved by, the state. The date filed must be specified.

In the case of an unincorporated association, the conformed copy of the constitution, articles of association, or other organizing document must indicate in the document itself, or in a written declaration, that the organization was formed by the adoption of the document by two or more persons.

If the organization has adopted bylaws, include a current copy. The bylaws need not be signed if submitted as an attachment to the application for recognition of exemption. The bylaws of an organization alone are not an organizing instrument. They are merely the internal rules and regulations of the organization.

In the case of a trust, a copy of the signed and dated trust instrument must be furnished.

For your organization to qualify for exempt status, its organizing instrument must contain a proper dissolution clause, or state law must provide for distribution of assets for one or more exempt (section 501(c)(3)) purposes upon dissolution. If you rely on state law, please cite the law and briefly state its provisions on an attachment. Foreign organizations must cite and attach a copy of the foreign statute along with an English language translation.

See Pub. 557 for a discussion of dissolution clauses under the heading, **Dedication and Distribution of Assets.** Examples of dissolution clauses are shown in the sample organizing instruments.

The organizing instrument must also specify the organizational purposes and the purposes specified must be limited to one or more of those set out in section 501(c)(3). See Pub. 557 for detailed instructions and for sample organizing instruments that satisfy the requirements of section 501(c)(3) and the related regulations.

Part II. Activities and Operational Information

Line 1.—It is important that you report all activities carried on by the organization to enable the IRS to make a proper determination of the organization's exempt status.

Line 2.—If it is anticipated that the organization's principal sources of support will increase or decrease substantially in relation to the organization's total support, attach a statement describing anticipated changes and explaining the basis for the expectation.

Line 3.—For purposes of providing the information requested on line 3, "fundraising activity" includes the solicitation of contributions and both functionally related activities and unrelated business activities. Include a description of the nature and magnitude of the activities.

Line 4a.—Furnish the mailing addresses of the organization's principal officers, directors, or trustees. Do not give the address of the organization.

Line 4b.—The annual compensation includes salary, bonus, and any other form of payment to the individual for services while employed by the organization.

Line 4c.—Public officials include anyone holding an elected position or anyone appointed to a position by an elected official.

Line 4d.—For purposes of this application, a "disqualified person" is any person who, if the applicant organization were a private foundation, is:

1. A "substantial contributor" to the foundation (defined below);
2. A foundation manager;
3. An owner of more than 20% of the total combined voting power of a corporation that is a substantial contributor to the foundation;
4. A "member of the family" of any person described in **1, 2,** or **3** above;
5. A corporation, partnership, or trust in which persons described in **1, 2, 3,** or **4** above, hold more than 35% of the combined voting power, the profits interest, or the beneficial interests; and
6. Any other private foundation that is effectively controlled by the same persons who control the first-mentioned private foundation or any other private foundation substantially all of whose contributions were made by the same contributors.

A substantial contributor is any person who gave a total of more than $5,000 to the organization, and those contributions are more than 2% of all the contributions and bequests received by the organization from the date it was created up to the end of the year the contributions by the substantial contributor were received. A creator of a trust is treated as a substantial contributor regardless of the amount contributed by that person or others.

See Pub. 578 for more information on "disqualified persons."

Line 5.—If your organization controls or is controlled by another exempt organization or a taxable organization, answer "Yes." "Control" means that:

1. Fifty percent (50%) or more of the filing organization's officers, directors, trustees, or key employees are also officers, directors, trustees, or key employees of the second organization being tested for control;
2. The filing organization appoints 50% or more of the officers, directors, trustees, or key employees of the second organization; or
3. Fifty percent (50%) or more of the filing organization's officers, directors, trustees, or key employees are appointed by the second organization.

Control exists if the 50% test is met by any one group of persons even if collectively the 50% test is not met. Examples of special relationships are common officers and the sharing of office space or employees.

Line 6.—If the organization conducts any financial transactions (either receiving funds or paying out funds), or nonfinancial activities with an exempt organization (other than a 501(c)(3) organization), or with a political organization, answer "Yes," and explain.

Line 7.—If the organization must report its income and expense activity to any other organization (tax-exempt or taxable entity), answer "Yes."

Line 8.—Examples of assets used to perform an exempt function are: land, building, equipment, and publications. Do not include cash or property producing investment income. If you have no assets used in performing the organization's exempt function, answer "N/A."

Line 10a.—If the organization is managed by another exempt organization, a taxable organization, or an individual, answer "Yes."

Line 10b.—If the organization leases property from anyone or leases any of its property to anyone, answer "Yes."

Line 11.—A membership organization for purposes of this question is an organization that is composed of individuals or organizations who:

   1. Share in the common goal for which the organization was created;

   2. Actively participate in achieving the organization's purposes; and

   3. Pay dues.

Line 12.—Examples of benefits, services, and products are: meals to homeless people, home for the aged, museum open to the public, and a symphony orchestra giving public performances.

Note: *Organizations that provide low-income housing should see Rev. Proc. 96-32, 1996-20 I.R.B. 14, for a "safe harbor" and an alternative facts and circumstances test to be used in completing line 12.*

Line 13.—An organization is attempting to influence legislation if it contacts or urges the public to contact members of a legislative body, for the purpose of proposing, supporting, or opposing legislation, or if it advocates the adoption or rejection of legislation.

If you answer "Yes," you may want to file **Form 5768,** Election/Revocation of Election by an Eligible Section 501(c)(3) Organization To Make Expenditures To Influence Legislation.

Line 14.—An organization is intervening in a political campaign if it promotes or opposes the candidacy or prospective candidacy of an individual for public office.

Part III. Technical Requirements

Line 1.—If you check "Yes," proceed to line 8. If you check "No," proceed to line 2.

Line 2a.—To qualify as an integrated auxiliary, an organization must not be a private foundation and must satisfy the affiliation and support tests of Regulations section 1.6033-2(h).

Line 3.—Relief from the 15-month filing requirement is granted automatically if the organization submits a completed Form 1023 within 12 months from the end of the 15-month period.

Line 4.—See Rev. Proc. 92-85, 1992-2 C.B. 490, for information about an extension beyond the 27-month period. According to section 5.01 of Rev. Proc. 92-85, the IRS will allow an organization an extension of time to file a Form 1023 application under a reasonable action and good-faith standard. In such case, the organization does not need to provide any further information or affidavits provided that it files its application before the IRS has discovered the organization's failure to file an application.

Line 5.—The reasons for late filing should be specific to your particular organization and situation. Rev. Proc. 92-85 lists the factors the IRS will consider in determining if good cause exists for granting an extension of time to file the application. (Also see Pub. 557.) To address these factors, your response on line 5 should provide the following information:

   1. Whether the organization consulted an attorney or accountant knowledgeable in tax matters or communicated with a responsible IRS employee (before or after the organization was created) to ascertain the organization's Federal filing requirements and, if so, the names and occupations or titles of the persons contacted, the approximate dates, and the substance of the information obtained;

   2. How and when the organization learned about the 15-month deadline for filing Form 1023;

   3. Whether any significant intervening circumstances beyond the organization's control prevented it from submitting the application timely or within a reasonable period of time after it learned of the requirement to file the application within the 15-month period; and

   4. Any other information that you believe may establish good cause for not filing timely or otherwise justify granting the relief sought.

Line 7.—The organization may still be able to qualify for exemption under section 501(c)(4) for the period preceding the effective date of its exemption as a section 501(c)(3) organization. If the organization is qualified under section 501(c)(4) and page 1 of Form 1024 is filed as directed, the organization will not be liable for income tax returns as a taxable entity. Contributions to section 501(c)(4) organizations are generally not deductible by donors as charitable contributions.

Line 8.—Private foundations are subject to various requirements, restrictions, and excise taxes under Chapter 42 of the Code that do not apply to public charities. Also, contributions to private foundations may receive less favorable treatment than contributions to public charities. See Pub. 578. Therefore, it is usually to an organization's advantage to show that it qualifies as a public charity rather than as a private foundation if its activities or sources of support permit it to do so. Unless an organization meets one of the exceptions below, it is a private foundation. In general, an organization is **not** a private foundation if it is:

   1. A church, school, hospital, or governmental unit;

   2. A medical research organization operated in conjunction with a hospital;

   3. An organization operated for the benefit of a college or university that is owned or operated by a governmental unit;

   4. An organization that normally receives a substantial part of its support in the form of contributions from a governmental unit or from the general public as provided in section 170(b)(1)(A)(vi);

   5. An organization that normally receives not more than one-third of its support from gross investment income and more than one-third of its support from contributions, membership fees, and gross receipts related to its exempt functions (subject to certain exceptions) as provided in section 509(a)(2);

   6. An organization operated solely for the benefit of, and in connection with, one or more of the organizations described above (or for the benefit of one or more of the organizations described in section 501(c)(4), (5), or (6) of the Code and also described in **5** above), but not controlled by disqualified persons other than foundation managers, as provided in section 509(a)(3); or

   7. An organization organized and operated to test for public safety as provided in section 509(a)(4).

Line 9.—Basis for private operating foundation status: (Complete this line **only** if you answered "Yes" to the question on line 8.)

A "private operating foundation" is a private foundation that spends substantially all of its adjusted net income or its minimum investment return, whichever is less, directly for the active conduct of the activities constituting the purpose or function for which it is organized and operated. The foundation must satisfy the income test and one of the three supplemental tests: **(1)** the assets test; **(2)** the endowment test; or **(3)** the support test. For additional information, see Pub. 578.

Line 10.—Basis for nonprivate foundation status: Check the box that shows why your organization is not a private foundation.

Box (a). A church or convention or association of churches.

Box (b). A school.—See the definition in the instructions for Schedule B.

Box (c). A hospital or medical research organization.—See the instructions for Schedule C.

Box (d). A governmental unit.—This category includes a state, a possession of the United States, or a political subdivision of any of the foregoing, or the United States, or the District of Columbia.

Box (e). Organizations operated in connection with or solely for organizations described in (a) through (d) or (g), (h), and (i).—The organization must be organized and operated for the benefit of, to perform the functions of, or to carry out the purposes of one or more specified organizations described in section 509(a)(1) or (2). It must be operated, supervised, or controlled by or in connection with one or more of the organizations described in the instructions for boxes **(a)** through **(d)** or **(g), (h),** and **(i)**. It must not be controlled directly or indirectly by disqualified persons (other than foundation managers or organizations described in section 509(a)(1) or (2)). To show whether the organization satisfies these tests, complete Schedule D.

Box (f). An organization testing for public safety.—An organization in this category is one that tests products to determine their acceptability for use by the general public. It does not include any organization testing for the benefit of a manufacturer as an operation or control in the manufacture of its product.

Box (g). Organization for the benefit of a college or university owned or operated by a governmental unit.—The organization must be organized and operated exclusively for the benefit of a college or university that is an educational organization within the meaning of section 170(b)(1)(A)(ii) and is an agency or instrumentality of a state or political subdivision of a state; is owned or operated by a state or political subdivision of a state; or is owned or operated by an agency or instrumentality of one or more states or political subdivisions. The organization must also normally receive a substantial part of its support from the United States or any state or political subdivision of a state, or from direct or indirect contributions from the general public or from a combination of these sources. An organizaton described in section 170(b)(1)(A)(iv) will be subject to the same publicly supported rules that are applicable to 170(b)(1)(A)(vi) organizations described in box (h) below.

Box (h). Organization receiving support from a governmental unit or from the general public.—The organization must receive a substantial part of its support from the United States or any state or political subdivision, or from direct or indirect contributions from the general public, or from a combination of these sources. The organization may satisfy the support requirement in either of two ways. It will be treated as publicly supported if the support it normally receives from the above-described governmental units and the general public equals at least one-third of its total support. It will also be treated as publicly supported if the support it normally receives from governmental or public sources equals at least 10% of total support and the organization is set up to attract new and additional public or governmental support on a continuous basis. If the organization's governmental and public support is at least 10%, but not over one-third of its total support, the questions on lines 1 through 14 of Part II will apply to determine both the organization's claim of exemption and whether it is publicly supported. Preparers should exercise care to assure that those questions are answered in detail.

Box (i). Organization described in section 509(a)(2).—The organization must satisfy the support test under section 509(a)(2)(A) and the gross investment income test under section 509(a)(2)(B). To satisfy the support test, the organization must normally receive more than one-third of its support from: **(a)** gifts, grants, contributions, or membership fees, and **(b)** gross receipts from admissions, sales of merchandise, performance of services, or furnishing of facilities, in an activity that is not an unrelated trade or business (subject to certain limitations discussed below). This one-third of support must be from organizations described in section 509(a)(1), governmental sources, or persons other than disqualified persons. In computing gross receipts from admissions, sales of merchandise, performance of services, or furnishing of facilities in an activity that is not an unrelated trade or business, the gross receipts from any one person or from any bureau or similar agency of a governmental unit are includible only to the extent they do not exceed the greater of $5,000 or 1% of the organization's total support. To satisfy the gross investment income test, the organization must not receive more than one-third of its support from gross investment income.

Box (j).—If you believe the organization meets the public support test of section 170(b)(1)(A)(vi) or 509(a)(2) but are uncertain as to which public support test it satisfies, check box (j). By checking this box, you are claiming that the organization is not a private foundation and are agreeing to let the IRS compute the public support of your organization and determine the correct foundation status.

Line 11.—To receive a definitive (final) ruling under sections 170(b)(1)(A)(vi) and 509(a)(1) or under section 509(a)(2), an organization must have completed a tax year consisting of at least 8 months. Organizations that checked box (h), (i), or (j) on line 10 that do not satisfy the 8-month requirement must request an advance ruling covering their first 5 tax years instead of a definitive ruling.

An organization that satisfies the 8-month requirement has two options:

1. It may request a definitive ruling. In this event, the organization's qualification under sections 170(b)(1)(A)(vi) and 509(a)(1) or under section 509(a)(2) will be based on the support that the organization has received to date; or

2. It may request an advance ruling. If the IRS issues the advance ruling, the organization's public support computation will be based on the support it receives during its first 5 tax years. An organization should consider this option if it has not received significant public support during its first tax year or during its first and second tax years, but it reasonably expects to receive such support by the end of its fifth tax year. An organization that receives an advance ruling is treated, during the 5-year advance ruling period, as a public charity (rather than a private foundation) for certain purposes, including those relating to the deductibility of contributions by the general public.

Line 12.—For definition of an unusual grant, see instructions for Part IV-A, line 12.

Line 13.—Answer this question only if you checked box (g), (h), or (j) on line 10.

Line 14.—Answer the question on this line only if you checked box (i) or (j) on line 10 and are requesting a definitive ruling on line 11.

Line 15.—Answer "Yes" or "No" on each line. If "Yes," you must complete the appropriate schedule. Each schedule is included in this application package with accompanying instructions. For a brief definition of each type of organization, see the appropriate schedule.

Part IV. Financial Data

The Statement of Revenue and Expenses must be completed **for the current year and each of the 3 years immediately before it** (or the years the organization has existed, if less than 4). Any applicant that has existed for less than 1 year must give financial data for the current year and proposed budgets for the following 2 years. We may request financial data for more than 4 years if necessary. All financial information for the current year must cover the period beginning on the first day of the organization's established annual accounting period and ending on any day that is within 60 days of the date of this application. If the date of this application is less than 60 days after the first day of the current accounting period, no financial information is required for the current year. Financial information is required for the 3 preceding years regardless of the current year requirements. Please note that if no financial information is required for the current year, the preceding year's financial information can end on any day that is within 60 days of the date of this application. Prepare the statements using the method of accounting and the accounting period (entered on line 4 of Part I) the organization uses in keeping its books and records. If the organization uses a method other than the cash receipts and disbursements method, attach a statement explaining the method used.

A. Statement of Revenue and Expenses

Line 1.—Do not include amounts received from the general public or a governmental unit for the exercise or performance of the organization's exempt functions. However, payments made by a governmental unit to enable the organization to provide a service to the general public should be included. Also, do not include unusual grants. For an explanation of unusual grants, see the discussion for **Line 12** on the following page.

Line 2.—Include amounts received from members for the basic purpose of providing support to the organization. These are considered to be contributions. Do not include payments to purchase admissions, merchandise, services, or use of facilities.

Line 3.—Include on this line the income received from dividends, interest, and payments received on securities loans, rents, and royalties.

Line 4.—Enter the organization's net income from any activities that are regularly carried on and are not related to the organization's exempt purposes. Examples of such income include fees from the commercial testing of products; income from renting office equipment or other personal property; and income from the sale of advertising in an exempt organization's periodical. See Pub. 598 for information about unrelated business income and activities.

Line 5.—Enter the amount collected by the local tax authority from the general public that has been allocated for your organization.

Line 6.—To report the value of services and/or facilities furnished by a governmental unit, use the fair market value at the time the service/facility was furnished to your organization. Do not include any other donated services or facilities in Part IV.

Line 7.—Enter the total income from all sources that is not reported on lines 1 through 6, or lines 9, 11, and 12. Attach a schedule that lists each type of revenue source and the amount derived from each.

Line 9.—Include income generated by the organization's exempt function activities (charitable, educational, etc.) and by its nontaxable fundraising events (excluding any contributions received). Examples of such income include the income derived by a symphony orchestra from the sale of tickets to its performances; and raffles, bingo, or other fundraising-event income that is not taxable as unrelated business income because the income-producing activities are not regularly carried on or because they are conducted with substantially all (at least 85%) volunteer labor. Record related cost of sales on line 22, Other.

Line 11.—Attach a schedule that shows a description of each asset, the name of the person to whom sold, and the amount received. In the case of publicly traded securities sold through a broker, the name of the purchaser is not required.

Line 12.—Unusual grants generally consist of substantial contributions and bequests from disinterested persons that:

1. Are attracted by reason of the publicly supported nature of the organization;

2. Are unusual and unexpected as to the amount; and

3. Would, by reason of their size, adversely affect the status of the organization as normally meeting the support test of section 170(b)(1)(A)(vi) or section 509(a)(2), as the case may be.

If the organization is awarded an unusual grant and the terms of the granting instrument provide that the organization will receive the funds over a period of years, the amount received by the organization each year under the grant may be excluded. See the regulations under sections 170 and 509.

Line 14.—Fundraising expenses represent the total expenses incurred in soliciting contributions, gifts, grants, etc.

Line 15.—Attach a schedule showing the name of the recipient, a brief description of the purposes or conditions of payment, and the amount paid. The following example shows the format and amount of detail required for this schedule:

Recipient	Purpose	Amount
Museum of Natural History	General operating budget	$9,000
State University	Books for needy students	4,500
Richard Roe	Educational scholarship	2,200

Colleges, universities, and other educational institutions and agencies subject to the Family Educational Rights and Privacy Act (20 U.S.C. 1232g) are not required to list the names of individuals who were provided scholarships or other financial assistance where such disclosure would violate the privacy provisions of the law. Instead, such organizations should group each type of financial aid provided, indicate the number of individuals who received the aid, and specify the aggregate dollar amount.

Line 16.—Attach a schedule showing the name of each recipient, a brief description of the purposes or condition of payment, and amount paid. Do not include any amounts that are on line 15. The schedule should be similar to the schedule shown in the line 15 instructions above.

Line 17.—Attach a schedule that shows the name of the person compensated; the office or position; the average amount of time devoted to the organization's affairs per week, month, etc.; and the amount of annual compensation. The following example shows the format and amount of detail required:

Name	Position	Time devoted	Annual salary
Philip Poe	President and general manager	16 hrs. per wk.	$7,500

Line 18.—Enter the total of employees' salaries not reported on line 17.

Line 19.—Enter the total interest expense for the year, excluding mortgage interest treated as occupancy expense on line 20.

Line 20.—Enter the amount paid for the use of office space or other facilities, heat, light, power, and other utilities, outside janitorial services, mortgage interest, real estate taxes, and similar expenses.

Line 21.—If your organization records depreciation, depletion, and similar expenses, enter the total.

Line 22.—Attach a schedule listing the type and amount of each **significant** expense for which a separate line is not provided. Report other miscellaneous expenses as a single total if not substantial in amount.

B. Balance Sheet

Line 1.—Enter the total cash in checking and savings accounts, temporary cash investments (money market funds, CDs, treasury bills, or other obligations that mature in less than 1 year), change funds, and petty cash funds.

Line 2.—Enter the total accounts receivable that arose from the sale of goods and/or performance of services, less any reserve for bad debt.

Line 3.—Enter the amount of materials, goods, and supplies purchased or manufactured by the organization and held to be sold or used in some future period.

Line 4.—Attach a schedule that shows the name of the borrower, a brief description of the obligation, the rate of return on the principal indebtedness, the due date, and the amount due. The following example shows the format and amount of detail required:

Name of borrower	Description of obligation	Rate of return	Due date	Amount
Hope Soap Corporation	Debenture bond (no senior issue outstanding)	10%	Jan. 2004	$ 7,500
Big Spool Company	Collateral note secured by company's fleet of 20 delivery trucks	12%	Jan. 2003	62,000

Line 5.—Attach a schedule listing the organization's corporate stock holdings. For stock of closely held corporations, the statement should show the name of the corporation, a brief summary of the corporation's capital structure, and the number of shares held and their value as carried on the organization's books. If such valuation does not reflect current fair market value, also include fair market value. For stock traded on an organized exchange or in substantial quantities over the counter, the statement should show the name of the corporation, a description of the stock and the principal exchange on which it is traded, the number of shares held, and their value as carried on the organization's books. The following example shows the format and the amount of detail required:

Name of corporation	Capital structure (or exchange on which traded)	Shares	Book amount	Fair market value
Little Spool Corporation	100 shares nonvoting preferred issued and outstanding, no par value; 50 shares common issued and outstanding, no par value.			
	Preferred shares:	50	$20,000	$24,000
	Common shares:	10	25,000	30,000
Flintlock Corporation	Class A common N.Y.S.E.	20	3,000	3,500

Line 6.—Report each loan separately, even if more than one loan was made to the same person. Attach a schedule that shows the borrower's name, purpose of loan, repayment terms, interest rate, and original amount of loan.

Line 7.—Enter the book value of government securities held (U.S., state, or municipal). Also enter the book value of buildings and equipment held for investment purposes. Attach a schedule identifying and reporting the book value of each.

Line 8.—Enter the book value of buildings and equipment **not** held for investment. This includes plant and equipment used by the organization in conducting its exempt activities. Attach a schedule listing these assets held at the end of the current tax year/period and the cost or other basis.

Line 9.—Enter the book value of land **not** held for investment.

Line 10.—Enter the book value of each category of assets not reported on lines 1 through 9. Attach a schedule listing each.

Line 12.—Enter the total of accounts payable to suppliers and others, such as salaries payable, accrued payroll taxes, and interest payable.

Line 13.—Enter the unpaid portion of grants and contributions that the organization has made a commitment to pay other organizations or individuals.

Line 14.—Enter the total of mortgages and other notes payable outstanding at the end of the current tax year/period. Attach a schedule that shows each item separately and the lender's name, purpose of loan, repayment terms, interest rate, and original amount.

Line 15.—Enter the amount of each liability not reported on lines 12 through 14. Attach a separate schedule.

Line 17.—Under fund accounting, an organization segregates its assets, liabilities, and net assets into separate funds according to restrictions on the use of certain assets. Each fund is like a separate entity in that it has a self-balancing set of accounts showing assets, liabilities, equity (fund balance), income, and expenses. If the organization does not use fund accounting, report only the "net assets" account balances, such as: capital stock, paid-in capital, and retained earnings or accumulated income.

Procedural Checklist

Make sure the application is complete.

If you do not complete all applicable parts or do not provide all required attachments, we may return the incomplete application to your organization for resubmission with the missing information or attachments. This will delay the processing of the application and may delay the effective date of your organization's exempt status. The organization may also incur additional user fees.

Have you . . .

_____ Attached **Form 8718** (User Fee for Exempt Organization Determination Letter Request) and the appropriate fee?

_____ Located the correct **IRS key district office** for the mailing of the application? (See **Where To File** addresses on Form 8718.) Do **not** file the application with your local Internal Revenue Service Center.

_____ Completed Parts I through IV and any other schedules that apply to the organization?

_____ Shown the organization's **Employer Identification Number (EIN)**?
a. If your organization has an EIN, write it in the space provided.
b. If this is a newly formed organization and does not have an Employer Identification Number, obtain an EIN by telephone. (See Specific Instructions, Part I, Line 2, on page 2.)

_____ Described your organization's **specific activities** as directed in Part II, line 1, of the application?

_____ Included a **conformed copy** of the complete organizing instrument? (See Specific Instructions, Part I, Line 11, on page 3.)

_____ Had the application signed by one of the following?
a. An officer or trustee who is authorized to sign (e.g., president, treasurer); **or**
b. A person authorized by a power of attorney (Submit Form 2848, or other power of attorney)

_____ Enclosed **financial statements** (Part IV)?
a. Current year (must include period up to within 60 days of the date the application is filed) and 3 preceding years.
b. Detailed breakdown of revenue and expenses (no lump sums).
c. If the organization has been in existence less than 1 year, you must also submit proposed budgets for 2 years showing the amounts and types of receipts and expenditures anticipated.

Note: *During the technical review of a completed application by the Employee Plans/Exempt Organizations Division in the key district or by Exempt Organizations Division in the National Office, it may be necessary to contact the organization for more specific or additional information.*

Do not send this checklist with the application.

Form **1023**
(Rev. April 1996)
Department of the Treasury
Internal Revenue Service

Application for Recognition of Exemption
Under Section 501(c)(3) of the Internal Revenue Code

OMB No. 1545-0056

If exempt status is approved, this application will be open for public inspection.

Read the instructions for each Part carefully.
A User Fee must be attached to this application.
If the required information and appropriate documents are not submitted along with Form 8718 (with payment of the appropriate user fee), the application may be returned to you.
Complete the Procedural Checklist on page 7 of the instructions.

Part I — Identification of Applicant

1a Full name of organization (as shown in organizing document)

2 Employer identification number (EIN) (If none, see page 2 of the instructions.)

1b c/o Name (if applicable)

3 Name and telephone number of person to be contacted if additional information is needed

1c Address (number and street) | Room/Suite

( )

1d City or town, state, and ZIP code

4 Month the annual accounting period ends

5 Date incorporated or formed | **6** Activity codes (See page 3 of the instructions.) | **7** Check here if applying under section:
a ☐ 501(e)   b ☐ 501(f)   c ☐ 501(k)

8 Did the organization previously apply for recognition of exemption under this Code section or under any other section of the Code? . . . . ☐ Yes ☐ No
If "Yes," attach an explanation.

9 Is the organization required to file Form 990 (or Form 990-EZ)? . . . . ☐ N/A ☐ Yes ☐ No
If "No," attach an explanation (see page 3 of the Specific Instructions).

10 Has the organization filed Federal income tax returns or exempt organization information returns? . . ☐ Yes ☐ No
If "Yes," state the form numbers, years filed, and Internal Revenue office where filed.

11 Check the box for the type of organization. ATTACH A CONFORMED COPY OF THE CORRESPONDING ORGANIZING DOCUMENTS TO THE APPLICATION BEFORE MAILING. (See **Specific Instructions for Part I, Line 11,** on page 3.) **Get Pub. 557, Tax-Exempt Status for Your Organization,** for examples of organizational documents.

a ☐ Corporation—Attach a copy of the Articles of Incorporation (including amendments and restatements) showing approval by the appropriate state official; also include a copy of the bylaws.

b ☐ Trust— Attach a copy of the Trust Indenture or Agreement, including all appropriate signatures and dates.

c ☐ Association— Attach a copy of the Articles of Association, Constitution, or other creating document, with a declaration (see instructions) or other evidence the organization was formed by adoption of the document by more than one person; also include a copy of the bylaws.

If the organization is a corporation or an unincorporated association that has not yet adopted bylaws, check here ▶ ☐

I declare under the penalties of perjury that I am authorized to sign this application on behalf of the above organization and that I have examined this application, including the accompanying schedules and attachments, and to the best of my knowledge it is true, correct, and complete.

Please Sign Here ▶ _____   _____   _____
(Signature)   (Title or authority of signer)   (Date)

For Paperwork Reduction Act Notice, see page 1 of the instructions.   Cat. No. 17133K

Form 1023 (Rev. 4-96) Page **2**

Part II — Activities and Operational Information

1 Provide a detailed narrative description of all the activities of the organization—past, present, and planned. **Do not merely refer to or repeat the language in the organizational document.** List each activity separately in the order of importance based on the relative time and other resources devoted to the activity. Indicate the percentage of time for each activity. Each description should include, as a minimum, the following: **(a)** a detailed description of the activity including its purpose and how each acitivity furthers your exempt purpose; **(b)** when the activity was or will be initiated; and **(c)** where and by whom the activity will be conducted.

2 What are or will be the organization's sources of financial support? List in order of size.

3 Describe the organization's fundraising program, both actual and planned, and explain to what extent it has been put into effect. Include details of fundraising activities such as selective mailings, formation of fundraising committees, use of volunteers or professional fundraisers, etc. Attach representative copies of solicitations for financial support.

Form 1023 (Rev. 4-96) Page **3**

Part II Activities and Operational Information *(Continued)*

4 Give the following information about the organization's governing body:

a Names, addresses, and titles of officers, directors, trustees, etc.	**b** Annual compensation

c Do any of the above persons serve as members of the governing body by reason of being public officials or being appointed by public officials? . . . . ☐ Yes ☐ No
If "Yes," name those persons and explain the basis of their selection or appointment.

d Are any members of the organization's governing body "disqualified persons" with respect to the organization (other than by reason of being a member of the governing body) or do any of the members have either a business or family relationship with "disqualified persons"? (See **Specific Instructions** for Part II, Line 4d, on page 3.) . . . . ☐ Yes ☐ No
If "Yes," explain.

5 Does the organization control or is it controlled by any other organization? . . . . ☐ Yes ☐ No

Is the organization the outgrowth of (or successor to) another organization, or does it have a special relationship with another organization by reason of interlocking directorates or other factors? . . . . ☐ Yes ☐ No
If either of these questions is answered "Yes," explain.

6 Does or will the organization directly or indirectly engage in any of the following transactions with any political organization or other exempt organization (other than a 501(c)(3) organization): **(a)** grants; **(b)** purchases or sales of assets; **(c)** rental of facilities or equipment; **(d)** loans or loan guarantees; **(e)** reimbursement arrangements; **(f)** performance of services, membership, or fundraising solicitations; or **(g)** sharing of facilities, equipment, mailing lists or other assets, or paid employees? . . . . . . ☐ Yes ☐ No
If "Yes," explain fully and identify the other organizations involved.

7 Is the organization financially accountable to any other organization? . . . . ☐ Yes ☐ No
If "Yes," explain and identify the other organization. Include details concerning accountability or attach copies of reports if any have been submitted.

Form 1023 (Rev. 4-96) Page **4**

Part II — Activities and Operational Information *(Continued)*

8 What assets does the organization have that are used in the performance of its exempt function? (Do not include property producing investment income.) If any assets are not fully operational, explain their status, what additional steps remain to be completed, and when such final steps will be taken. If "None," indicate "N/A."

9 Will the organization be the beneficiary of tax-exempt bond financing within the next 2 years? . . . ☐ Yes ☐ No

10a Will any of the organization's facilities or operations be managed by another organization or individual under a contractual agreement? . . . ☐ Yes ☐ No

b Is the organization a party to any leases? . . . ☐ Yes ☐ No

If either of these questions is answered "Yes," attach a copy of the contracts and explain the relationship between the applicant and the other parties.

11 Is the organization a membership organization? . . . ☐ Yes ☐ No
If "Yes," complete the following:

a Describe the organization's membership requirements and attach a schedule of membership fees and dues.

b Describe the organization's present and proposed efforts to attract members and attach a copy of any descriptive literature or promotional material used for this purpose.

c What benefits do (or will) the members receive in exchange for their payment of dues?

12a If the organization provides benefits, services, or products, are the recipients required, or will they be required, to pay for them? . . . ☐ N/A ☐ Yes ☐ No
If "Yes," explain how the charges are determined and attach a copy of the current fee schedule.

b Does or will the organization limit its benefits, services, or products to specific individuals or classes of individuals? . . . ☐ N/A ☐ Yes ☐ No
If "Yes," explain how the recipients or beneficiaries are or will be selected.

13 Does or will the organization attempt to influence legislation? . . . ☐ Yes ☐ No
If "Yes," explain. Also, give an estimate of the percentage of the organization's time and funds that it devotes or plans to devote to this activity.

14 Does or will the organization intervene in any way in political campaigns, including the publication or distribution of statements? . . . ☐ Yes ☐ No
If "Yes," explain fully.

Form 1023 (Rev. 4-96) Page **5**

Part III Technical Requirements

1 Are you filing Form 1023 within 15 months from the end of the month in which your organization was created or formed? . . . . ☐ **Yes** ☐ **No**

If you answer "Yes," do not answer questions on lines 2 through 7 below.

---

2 If one of the exceptions to the 15-month filing requirement shown below applies, check the appropriate box and proceed to question 8.

Exceptions—You are not required to file an exemption application within 15 months if the organization:

☐ **a** Is a church, interchurch organization of local units of a church, a convention or association of churches, or an integrated auxiliary of a church. See Specific Instructions, Line 2a, on page 4;

☐ **b** Is not a private foundation and normally has gross receipts of not more than $5,000 in each tax year; or

☐ **c** Is a subordinate organization covered by a group exemption letter, but only if the parent or supervisory organization timely submitted a notice covering the subordinate.

---

3 If the organization does not meet any of the exceptions on line 2 above, are you filing Form 1023 within 27 months from the end of the month in which the organization was created or formed? . . . . . . ☐ **Yes** ☐ **No**

If "Yes," your organization qualifies under section 4.01 of Rev. Proc. 92-85, 1992-2 C.B. 490, for an automatic 12-month extension of the 15-month filing requirement. Do not answer questions 4 through 7.

If "No," answer question 4.

---

4 If you answer "No" to question 3, has the organization been contacted by the IRS regarding its failure to file Form 1023 within 27 months from the end of the month in which the organization was created or formed? . . . . ☐ **Yes** ☐ **No**

If "No," your organization is requesting an extension of time to apply under the "reasonable action and good faith" requirements of section 5.01 of Rev. Proc. 92-85. Do not answer questions 5 through 7.

If "Yes," answer question 5.

---

5 If you answer "Yes" to question 4, does the organization wish to request relief from the 15-month filing requirement? . . . . ☐ **Yes** ☐ **No**

If "Yes," give the reasons for not filing this application prior to being contacted by the IRS. See Specific Instructions, Line 5, on page 4 before completing this item. Do not answer questions 6 and 7.

If "No," answer question 6.

---

6 If you answer "No" to question 5, your organization's qualification as a section 501(c)(3) organization can be recognized only from the date this application is filed with your key District Director. Therefore, do you want us to consider the application as a request for recognition of exemption as a section 501(c)(3) organization from the date the application is received and not retroactively to the date the organization was created or formed? . . . . ☐ **Yes** ☐ **No**

---

7 If you answer "Yes" to question 6 above and wish to request recognition of section 501(c)(4) status for the period beginning with the date the organization was formed and ending with the date the Form 1023 application was received (the effective date of the organization's section 501(c)(3) status), check here ▶ ☐ and attach a completed page 1 of Form 1024 to this application.

Form 1023 (Rev. 4-96) Page **6**

Part III Technical Requirements *(Continued)*

8 Is the organization a private foundation?
☐ **Yes** (Answer question 9.)
☐ **No** (Answer question 10 and proceed as instructed.)

9 If you answer "Yes" to question 8, does the organization claim to be a private operating foundation?
☐ **Yes** (Complete Schedule E.)
☐ **No**

After answering question 9 on this line, go to line 15 on page 7.

10 If you answer "No" to question 8, indicate the public charity classification the organization is requesting by checking the box below that most appropriately applies:

THE ORGANIZATION IS NOT A PRIVATE FOUNDATION BECAUSE IT QUALIFIES:

a	☐	As a church or a convention or association of churches (CHURCHES MUST COMPLETE SCHEDULE A.)	Sections 509(a)(1) and 170(b)(1)(A)(i)
b	☐	As a school (MUST COMPLETE SCHEDULE B.)	Sections 509(a)(1) and 170(b)(1)(A)(ii)
c	☐	As a hospital or a cooperative hospital service organization, or a medical research organization operated in conjunction with a hospital (MUST COMPLETE SCHEDULE C.)	Sections 509(a)(1) and 170(b)(1)(A)(iii)
d	☐	As a governmental unit described in section 170(c)(1).	Sections 509(a)(1) and 170(b)(1)(A)(v)
e	☐	As being operated solely for the benefit of, or in connection with, one or more of the organizations described in **a** through **d**, **g**, **h**, or **i** (MUST COMPLETE SCHEDULE D.)	Section 509(a)(3)
f	☐	As being organized and operated exclusively for testing for public safety.	Section 509(a)(4)
g	☐	As being operated for the benefit of a college or university that is owned or operated by a governmental unit.	Sections 509(a)(1) and 170(b)(1)(A)(iv)
h	☐	As receiving a substantial part of its support in the form of contributions from publicly supported organizations, from a governmental unit, or from the general public.	Sections 509(a)(1) and 170(b)(1)(A)(vi)
i	☐	As normally receiving not more than one-third of its support from gross investment income and more than one-third of its support from contributions, membership fees, and gross receipts from activities related to its exempt functions (subject to certain exceptions).	Section 509(a)(2)
j	☐	The organization is a publicly supported organization but is not sure whether it meets the public support test of block **h** or block **i**. The organization would like the IRS to decide the proper classification.	Sections 509(a)(1) and 170(b)(1)(A)(vi) or Section 509(a)(2)

If you checked one of the boxes **a** through **f** in question 10, go to question 15. If you checked box **g** in question 10, go to questions 12 and 13.
If you checked box **h**, **i**, or **j**, in question 10, go to question 11.

Form 1023 (Rev. 4-96) Page **7**

Part III — Technical Requirements *(Continued)*

11 If you checked box **h, i,** or **j** in question 10, has the organization completed a tax year of at least 8 months?
- ☐ Yes—Indicate whether you are requesting:
  - ☐ A definitive ruling (Answer questions 12 through 15.)
  - ☐ An advance ruling (Answer questions 12 and 15 and attach two Forms 872-C completed and signed.)
- ☐ No—**You must request an advance ruling by completing and signing two Forms 872-C and attaching them to the application.**

12 If the organization received any unusual grants during any of the tax years shown in Part IV-A, attach a list for each year showing the name of the contributor; the date and the amount of the grant; and a brief description of the nature of the grant.

13 If you are requesting a definitive ruling under section 170(b)(1)(A)(iv) or (vi), check here ▶ ☐ and:

  a Enter 2% of line 8, column (e), Total, of Part IV-A. _____

  b Attach a list showing the name and amount contributed by each person (other than a governmental unit or "publicly supported" organization) whose total gifts, grants, contributions, etc., were more than the amount entered on line **13a** above.

14 If you are requesting a definitive ruling under section 509(a)(2), check here ▶ ☐ and:

  a For each of the years included on lines 1, 2, and 9 of Part IV-A, attach a list showing the name of and amount received from each "disqualified person." (For a definition of "disqualified person," see **Specific Instructions,** Part II, Line 4d, on page 3.)

  b For each of the years included on line 9 of Part IV-A, attach a list showing the name of and amount received from each payer (other than a "disqualified person") whose payments to the organization were more than $5,000. For this purpose, "payer" includes, but is not limited to, any organization described in sections 170(b)(1)(A)(i) through (vi) and any governmental agency or bureau.

15 Indicate if your organization is one of the following. If so, complete the required schedule. (Submit only those schedules that apply to your organization. **Do not submit blank schedules.**)

	Yes	No	If "Yes," complete Schedule:
Is the organization a church?			A
Is the organization, or any part of it, a school?			B
Is the organization, or any part of it, a hospital or medical research organization?			C
Is the organization a section 509(a)(3) supporting organization?			D
Is the organization a private operating foundation?			E
Is the organization, or any part of it, a home for the aged or handicapped?			F
Is the organization, or any part of it, a child care organization?			G
Does the organization provide or administer any scholarship benefits, student aid, etc.?			H
Has the organization taken over, or will it take over, the facilities of a "for profit" institution?			I

Form 1023 (Rev. 4-96) Page **8**

Part IV Financial Data

Complete the financial statements for the current year and for each of the 3 years immediately before it. If in existence less than 4 years, complete the statements for each year in existence. **If in existence less than 1 year, also provide proposed budgets for the 2 years following the current year.**

A. Statement of Revenue and Expenses

		Current tax year	3 prior tax years or proposed budget for 2 years			
		(a) From .... to	**(b)** 19........	**(c)** 19........	**(d)** 19........	**(e) TOTAL**
Revenue	1 Gifts, grants, and contributions received (not including unusual grants—see pages 5 and 6 of the instructions)					
	2 Membership fees received					
	3 Gross investment income (see instructions for definition)					
	4 Net income from organization's unrelated business activities not included on line 3					
	5 Tax revenues levied for and either paid to or spent on behalf of the organization					
	6 Value of services or facilities furnished by a governmental unit to the organization without charge (not including the value of services or facilities generally furnished the public without charge)					
	7 Other income (not including gain or loss from sale of capital assets) (attach schedule)					
	8 **Total** (add lines 1 through 7)					
	9 Gross receipts from admissions, sales of merchandise or services, or furnishing of facilities in any activity that is not an unrelated business within the meaning of section 513. Include related cost of sales on line 22					
	10 **Total** (add lines 8 and 9)					
	11 Gain or loss from sale of capital assets (attach schedule)					
	12 Unusual grants					
	13 **Total** revenue (add lines 10 through 12)					
Expenses	14 Fundraising expenses					
	15 Contributions, gifts, grants, and similar amounts paid (attach schedule)					
	16 Disbursements to or for benefit of members (attach schedule)					
	17 Compensation of officers, directors, and trustees (attach schedule)					
	18 Other salaries and wages					
	19 Interest					
	20 Occupancy (rent, utilities, etc.)					
	21 Depreciation and depletion					
	22 Other (attach schedule)					
	23 **Total** expenses (add lines 14 through 22)					
	24 Excess of revenue over expenses (line 13 minus line 23)					

Form 1023 (Rev. 4-96) Page **9**

Part IV — Financial Data *(Continued)*

B. Balance Sheet (at the end of the period shown)

Current tax year
Date ....

Assets

1	Cash	1
2	Accounts receivable, net	2
3	Inventories	3
4	Bonds and notes receivable (attach schedule)	4
5	Corporate stocks (attach schedule)	5
6	Mortgage loans (attach schedule)	6
7	Other investments (attach schedule)	7
8	Depreciable and depletable assets (attach schedule)	8
9	Land	9
10	Other assets (attach schedule)	10
11	**Total assets** (add lines 1 through 10)	11

Liabilities

12	Accounts payable	12
13	Contributions, gifts, grants, etc., payable	13
14	Mortgages and notes payable (attach schedule)	14
15	Other liabilities (attach schedule)	15
16	**Total liabilities** (add lines 12 through 15)	16

Fund Balances or Net Assets

17	Total fund balances or net assets	17
18	**Total liabilities and fund balances or net assets** (add line 16 and line 17)	18

If there has been any substantial change in any aspect of the organization's financial activities since the end of the period shown above, check the box and attach a detailed explanation ▶ ☐

Form **872-C**

(Rev. April 1996)

Department of the Treasury
Internal Revenue Service

Consent Fixing Period of Limitation Upon Assessment of Tax Under Section 4940 of the Internal Revenue Code

(See instructions on reverse side.)

OMB No. 1545-0056

To be used with Form 1023. Submit in duplicate.

Under section 6501(c)(4) of the Internal Revenue Code, and as part of a request filed with Form 1023 that the organization named below be treated as a publicly supported organization under section 170(b)(1)(A)(vi) or section 509(a)(2) during an advance ruling period,

----
(Exact legal name of organization as shown in organizing document)

(Number, street, city or town, state, and ZIP code)

and the

District Director of Internal Revenue, or Assistant Commissioner (Employee Plans and Exempt Organizations)

Consent and agree that the period for assessing tax (imposed under section 4940 of the Code) for any of the 5 tax years in the advance ruling period will extend 8 years, 4 months, and 15 days beyond the end of the first tax year.

However, if a notice of deficiency in tax for any of these years is sent to the organization before the period expires, the time for making an assessment will be further extended by the number of days the assessment is prohibited, plus 60 days.

Ending date of first tax year ------------------------------------
(Month, day, and year)

Name of organization (as shown in organizing document)	Date
Officer or trustee having authority to sign	
Signature ▶	Title ▶

For IRS use only

District Director or Assistant Commissioner (Employee Plans and Exempt Organizations)	Date
By ▶	

For Paperwork Reduction Act Notice, see page 1 of the Form 1023 Instructions. Cat. No. 16905Q

You must complete this form and attach it to the Form 1023 if you checked box **h, i,** or **j** of Part III, question 10, and the organization has not completed a tax year of at least 8 months.

> For example: If the organization incorporated May 15 and its year ends December 31, it has completed a tax year of only 7½ months. Therefore, Form 872-C must be submitted.

(a) Enter the name of the organization. This must be entered exactly as it appears in the organizing document. Do not use abbreviations unless the organizing document does.

(b) Enter the current address.

(c) Enter the ending date of the first tax year.

> For example:
> (1) If the organization was formed on June 15 and it has chosen December 31 as its year end, enter December 31, 19 _____.
> (2) If the organization was formed June 15 and it has chosen June 30 as its year end, enter June 30, 19 _____. In this example, the organization's first tax year consists of only 15 days.

(d) The form must be signed by an authorized officer or trustee, generally the president or treasurer.

(e) Enter the date that the form was signed.

DO NOT MAKE ANY OTHER ENTRIES.

Schedule D. Section 509(a)(3) Supporting Organizations

1a Organizations supported by the applicant organization:
Name and address of supported organization

b Has the supported organization received a ruling or determination letter that it is not a private foundation by reason of section 509(a)(1) or (2)?

Name and address		
	☐ Yes	☐ No
	☐ Yes	☐ No
	☐ Yes	☐ No
	☐ Yes	☐ No
	☐ Yes	☐ No

c If "No" for any of the organizations listed in **1a**, explain.

2 Does the supported organization have tax-exempt status under section 501(c)(4), 501(c)(5), or 501(c)(6)? ☐ Yes ☐ No
If "Yes," attach: **(a)** a copy of its ruling or determination letter, and **(b)** an analysis of its revenue for the current year and the preceding 3 years. (Provide the financial data using the formats in Part IV-A (lines 1–13) and Part III (lines 12, 13, and 14).)

3 Does your organization's governing document indicate that the majority of its governing board is elected or appointed by the supported organizations? ☐ Yes ☐ No
If "Yes," skip to line 9.
If "No," you must answer the questions on lines 4 through 9.

4 Does your organization's governing document indicate the common supervision or control that it and the supported organizations share? ☐ Yes ☐ No
If "Yes," give the article and paragraph numbers. If "No," explain.

5 To what extent do the supported organizations have a significant voice in your organization's investment policies, in the making and timing of grants, and in otherwise directing the use of your organization's income or assets?

6 Does the mentioning of the supported organizations in your organization's governing instrument make it a trust that the supported organizations can enforce under state law and compel to make an accounting? ☐ Yes ☐ No
If "Yes," explain.

7a What percentage of your organization's income does it pay to each supported organization?

b What is the total annual income of each supported organization?

c How much does your organization contribute annually to each supported organization?

For more information, see back of Schedule D.

Schedule D. Section 509(a)(3) Supporting Organizations *(Continued)*

8 To what extent does your organization conduct activities that would otherwise be carried on by the supported organizations? Explain why these activities would otherwise be carried on by the supported organizations.

9 Is the applicant organization controlled directly or indirectly by one or more "disqualified persons" (other than one who is a disqualified person solely because he or she is a manager) or by an organization that is not described in section 509(a)(1) or (2)? . . . . ☐ Yes ☐ No
If "Yes," explain.

Instructions

For an explanation of the types of organizations defined in section 509(a)(3) as being excluded from the definition of a private foundation, see Pub. 557, Chapter 3.

Line 1

List each organization that is supported by your organization and indicate in item **1b** if the supported organization has received a letter recognizing exempt status as a section 501(c)(3) public charity as defined in section 509(a)(1) or 509(a)(2). If you answer "No" in **1b** to any of the listed organizations, please explain in **1c.**

Line 3

Your organization's governing document may be articles of incorporation, articles of association, constitution, trust indenture, or trust agreement.

Line 9

For a definition of a "disqualified person," see **Specific Instructions,** Part II, Line 4d, on page 3 of the application's instructions.

Schedule E. Private Operating Foundations

		Most recent tax year
Income Test		
1a Adjusted net income, as defined in Regulations section 53.4942(a)-2(d)	1a	
b Minimum investment return, as defined in Regulations section 53.4942(a)-2(c)	1b	
2 Qualifying distributions:		
a Amounts (including administrative expenses) paid directly for the active conduct of the activities for which organized and operated under section 501(c)(3) (attach schedule)	2a	
b Amounts paid to acquire assets to be used (or held for use) directly in carrying out purposes described in section 170(c)(1) or 170(c)(2)(B) (attach schedule)	2b	
c Amounts set aside for specific projects that are for purposes described in section 170(c)(1) or 170(c)(2)(B) (attach schedule)	2c	
d **Total** qualifying distributions (add lines 2a, b, and c)	2d	
3 Percentages:		
a Percentage of qualifying distributions to adjusted net income (divide line 2d by line 1a)	3a	%
b Percentage of qualifying distributions to minimum investment return (divide line 2d by line 1b) (Percentage must be at least 85% for 3a or 3b)	3b	%
Assets Test		
4 Value of organization's assets used in activities that directly carry out the exempt purposes. Do not include assets held merely for investment or production of income (attach schedule)	4	
5 Value of any stock of a corporation that is controlled by applicant organization and carries out its exempt purposes (attach statement describing corporation)	5	
6 Value of all qualifying assets (add lines 4 and 5)	6	
7 Value of applicant organization's total assets	7	
8 Percentage of qualifying assets to total assets (divide line 6 by line 7—percentage must exceed 65%)	8	%
Endowment Test		
9 Value of assets not used (or held for use) directly in carrying out exempt purposes:		
a Monthly average of investment securities at fair market value	9a	
b Monthly average of cash balances	9b	
c Fair market value of all other investment property (attach schedule)	9c	
d **Total** (add lines 9a, b, and c)	9d	
10 Acquisition indebtedness related to line 9 items (attach schedule)	10	
11 Balance (subtract line 10 from line 9d)	11	
12 Multiply line 11 by 3⅓% (⅔ of the percentage for the minimum investment return computation under section 4942(e)). Line 2d above must equal or exceed the result of this computation	12	
Support Test		
13 Applicant organization's support as defined in section 509(d)	13	
14 Gross investment income as defined in section 509(e)	14	
15 Support for purposes of section 4942(j)(3)(B)(iii) (subtract line 14 from line 13)	15	
16 Support received from the general public, five or more exempt organizations, or a combination of these sources (attach schedule)	16	
17 For persons (other than exempt organizations) contributing more than 1% of line 15, enter the total amounts that are more than 1% of line 15	17	
18 Subtract line 17 from line 16	18	
19 Percentage of total support (divide line 18 by line 15—must be at least 85%)	19	%
20 Does line 16 include support from an exempt organization that is more than 25% of the amount of line 15?	☐ Yes ☐ No	

21 Newly created organizations with less than 1 year's experience: Attach a statement explaining how the organization is planning to satisfy the requirements of section 4942(j)(3) for the income test and one of the supplemental tests during its first year's operation. Include a description of plans and arrangements, press clippings, public announcements, solicitations for funds, etc.

22 Does the amount entered on line 2a above include any grants that the applicant organization made?   ☐ Yes ☐ No
If "Yes," attach a statement explaining how those grants satisfy the criteria for "significant involvement" grants described in section 53.4942(b)-1(b)(2) of the regulations.

For more information, see back of Schedule E.

Instructions

If the organization claims to be an operating foundation described in section 4942(j)(3) and—

a. Bases its claim to private operating foundation status on normal and regular operations over a period of years; or

b. Is newly created, set up as a private operating foundation, and has at least 1 year's experience;

provide the information under the **income test and under one of the three supplemental tests** (assets, endowment, or support). If the organization does not have at least 1 year's experience, provide the information called for on line 21. If the organization's private operating foundation status depends on its normal and regular operations as described in **a** above, attach a schedule similar to Schedule E showing the data in tabular form for the 3 years preceding the most recent tax year. (See Regulations section 53.4942(b)-1 for additional information before completing the "Income Test" section of this schedule.) Organizations claiming section 4942(j)(5) status must satisfy the income test and the endowment test.

A "private operating foundation" described in section 4942(j)(3) is a private foundation that spends substantially all of the smaller of its adjusted net income (as defined below) or its minimum investment return directly for the active conduct of the activities constituting the purpose or function for which it is organized and operated. The foundation must satisfy the income test under section 4942(j)(3)(A), as modified by Regulations section 53.4942(b)-1, and one of the following three supplemental tests: **(1)** the assets test under section 4942(j)(3)(B)(i); **(2)** the endowment test under section 4942(j)(3)(B)(ii); or **(3)** the support test under section 4942(j)(3)(B)(iii).

Certain long-term care facilities described in section 4942(j)(5) are treated as private operating foundations for purposes of section 4942 only.

"Adjusted net income" is the excess of gross income determined with the income modifications described below for the tax year over the sum of deductions determined with the deduction modifications described below. Items of gross income from any unrelated trade or business and the deductions directly connected with the unrelated trade or business are taken into account in computing the organization's adjusted net income.

Income Modifications

The following are income modifications (adjustments to gross income):

1. Section 103 (relating to interest on certain governmental obligations) does not apply. Thus, interest that otherwise would have been excluded should be included in gross income.

2. Except as provided in **3** below, capital gains and losses are taken into account only to the extent of the net short-term gain. Long-term gains and losses are disregarded.

3. The gross amount received from the sale or disposition of certain property should be included in gross income to the extent that the acquisition of the property constituted a qualifying distribution under section 4942(g)(1)(B).

4. Repayments of prior qualifying distributions (as defined in section 4942(g)(1)(A)) constitute items of gross income.

5. Any amount set aside under section 4942(g)(2) that is "not necessary for the purposes for which it was set aside" constitutes an item of gross income.

Deduction Modifications

The following are deduction modifications (adjustments to deductions):

1. Expenses for the general operation of the organization according to its charitable purposes (as contrasted with expenses for the production or collection of income and management, conservation, or maintenance of income-producing property) should not be taken as deductions. If only a portion of the property is used for production of income subject to section 4942 and the remainder is used for general charitable purposes, the expenses connected with that property should be divided according to those purposes. Only expenses related to the income-producing portion should be taken as deductions.

2. Charitable contributions, deductible under section 170 or 642(c), should not be taken into account as deductions for adjusted net income.

3. The net operating loss deduction prescribed under section 172 should not be taken into account as a deduction for adjusted net income.

4. The special deductions for corporations (such as the dividends-received deduction) allowed under sections 241 through 249 should not be taken into account as deductions for adjusted net income.

5. Depreciation and depletion should be determined in the same manner as under section 4940(c)(3)(B).

Section 265 (relating to the expenses and interest connected with tax-exempt income) should not be taken into account.

You may find it easier to figure adjusted net income by completing column (c), Part 1, Form 990-PF, according to the instructions for that form.

An organization that has been held to be a private operating foundation will continue to be such an organization only if it meets the income test and either the assets, endowment, or support test in later years. See Regulations section 53.4942(b) for additional information. No additional request for ruling will be necessary or appropriate for an organization to maintain its status as a private operating foundation. However, data related to the above tests must be submitted with the organization's annual information return, Form 990-PF.

Form 1023 (Rev. 4-96) Page **27**

Schedule H. Organizations Providing Scholarship Benefits, Student Aid, etc., to Individuals

1a Describe the nature and the amount of the scholarship benefit, student aid, etc., including the terms and conditions governing its use, whether a gift or a loan, and how the availability of the scholarship is publicized. If the organization has established or will establish several categories of scholarship benefits, identify each kind of benefit and explain how the organization determines the recipients for each category. Attach a sample copy of any application the organization requires individuals to complete to be considered for scholarship grants, loans, or similar benefits. (Private foundations that make grants for travel, study, or other similar purposes are required to obtain advance approval of scholarship procedures. See Regulations sections 53.4945-4(c) and (d).)

b If you want this application considered as a request for approval of grant procedures in the event we determine that the organization is a private foundation, check here . . . . ▶ ☐

c If you checked the box in 1b above, check the boxes for which you wish the organization to be considered.

☐ 4945(g)(1)   ☐ 4945(g)(2)   ☐ 4945(g)(3)

2 What limitations or restrictions are there on the class of individuals who are eligible recipients? Specifically explain whether there are, or will be, any restrictions or limitations in the selection procedures based upon race or the employment status of the prospective recipient or any relative of the prospective recipient. Also indicate the approximate number of eligible individuals.

3 Indicate the number of grants the organization anticipates making annually . . . . ▶

4 If the organization bases its selections in any way on the employment status of the applicant or any relative of the applicant, indicate whether there is or has been any direct or indirect relationship between the members of the selection committee and the employer. Also indicate whether relatives of the members of the selection committee are possible recipients or have been recipients.

5 Describe any procedures the organization has for supervising grants (such as obtaining reports or transcripts) that it awards and any procedures it has for taking action if the terms of the grant are violated.

For more information, see back of Schedule H.

Additional Information

Private foundations that make grants to individuals for travel, study, or other similar purposes are required to obtain advance approval of their grant procedures from the IRS. Such grants that are awarded under selection procedures that have not been approved by the IRS are subject to a 10% excise tax under section 4945. (See Regulations sections 53.4945-4(c) and (d).)

If you are requesting advance approval of the organization's grant procedures, the following sections apply to line 1c:

4945(g)(1)—The grant constitutes a scholarship or fellowship grant that meets the provisions of section 117(a) prior to its amendment by the Tax Reform Act of 1986 and is to be used for study at an educational organization (school) described in section 170(b)(1)(A)(ii).

4945(g)(2)—The grant constitutes a prize or award that is subject to the provisions of section 74(b), if the recipient of such a prize or award is selected from the general public.

4945(g)(3)—The purpose of the grant is to achieve a specific objective, produce a report or other similar product, or improve or enhance a literary, artistic, musical, scientific, teaching, or other similar capacity, skill, or talent of the grantee.

Schedule I. Successors to "For Profit" Institutions

1 What was the name of the predecessor organization and the nature of its activities?

2 Who were the owners or principal stockholders of the predecessor organization? (If more space is needed, attach schedule.)

Name and address	Share or interest

3 Describe the business or family relationship between the owners or principal stockholders and principal employees of the predecessor organization and the officers, directors, and principal employees of the applicant organization.

4a Attach a copy of the agreement of sale or other contract that sets forth the terms and conditions of sale of the predecessor organization or of its assets to the applicant organization.

b Attach an appraisal by an independent qualified expert showing the fair market value at the time of sale of the facilities or property interest sold.

5 Has any property or equipment formerly used by the predecessor organization been rented to the applicant organization or will any such property be rented? . . . . ☐ Yes ☐ No
If "Yes," explain and attach copies of all leases and contracts.

6 Is the organization leasing or will it lease or otherwise make available any space or equipment to the owners, principal stockholders, or principal employees of the predecessor organization? . . . . . . ☐ Yes ☐ No
If "Yes," explain and attach a list of these tenants and a copy of the lease for each such tenant.

7 Were any new operating policies initiated as a result of the transfer of assets from a profit-making organization to a nonprofit organization? . . . . ☐ Yes ☐ No
If "Yes," explain.

Additional Information

A "for profit" institution for purposes of Schedule I includes any organization in which a person may have a proprietary or partnership interest, hold corporate stock, or otherwise exercise an ownership interest. The institution need not have operated for the purpose of making a profit.

Activity Code Numbers of Exempt Organizations (select up to three codes that best describe or most accurately identify your organization's purposes, activities, operations or type of organization and enter in block 6, page 1, of the application. Enter first the code that most accurately identifies the organization.)

Code

Religious Activities

001 Church, synagogue, etc.
002 Association or convention of churches
003 Religious order
004 Church auxiliary
005 Mission
006 Missionary activities
007 Evangelism
008 Religious publishing activities
--- Bookstore (use 918)
--- Genealogical activities (use 094)
029 Other religious activities

Schools, Colleges, and Related Activities

030 School, college, trade school, etc.
031 Special school for the blind, handicapped, etc.
032 Nursery school
--- Day care center (use 574)
033 Faculty group
034 Alumni association or group
035 Parent or parent-teachers association
036 Fraternity or sorority
--- Key club (use 323)
037 Other student society or group
038 School or college athletic association
039 Scholarships for children of employees
040 Scholarships (other)
041 Student loans
042 Student housing activities
043 Other student aid
044 Student exchange with foreign country
045 Student operated business
--- Financial support of schools, colleges, etc. (use 602)
--- Achievement prizes or awards (use 914)
--- Student bookstore (use 918)
--- Student travel (use 299)
--- Scientific research (see Scientific Research Activities)
046 Private school
059 Other school related activities

Cultural, Historical or Other Educational Activities

060 Museum, zoo, planetarium, etc.
061 Library
062 Historical site, records, or reenactment
063 Monument
064 Commemorative event (centennial, festival, pageant, etc.)
065 Fair
088 Community theatrical group
089 Singing society or group
090 Cultural performances
091 Art exhibit
092 Literary activities
093 Cultural exchanges with foreign country
094 Genealogical activities
--- Achievement prizes or awards (use 914)
--- Gifts or grants to individuals (use 561)
--- Financial support of cultural organizations (use 602)
119 Other cultural or historical activities

Other Instruction and Training Activities

120 Publishing activities
121 Radio or television broadcasting
122 Producing films
123 Discussion groups, forums, panels, lectures, etc.
124 Study and research (nonscientific)
125 Giving information or opinion (see also Advocacy)
126 Apprentice training
--- Travel tours (use 299)
149 Other instruction and training

Health Services and Related Activities

150 Hospital
151 Hospital auxiliary
152 Nursing or convalescent home
153 Care and housing for the aged (see also 382)
154 Health clinic
155 Rural medical facility
156 Blood bank
157 Cooperative hospital service organization
158 Rescue and emergency service
159 Nurses register or bureau
160 Aid to the handicapped (see also 031)
161 Scientific research (diseases)
162 Other medical research
163 Health insurance (medical, dental, optical, etc.)
164 Prepared group health plan
165 Community health planning
166 Mental health care
167 Group medical practice association
168 In-faculty group practice association
169 Hospital pharmacy, parking facility, food services, etc.
179 Other health services

Scientific Research Activities

180 Contract or sponsored scientific research for industry

Code

181 Scientific research for government
--- Scientific research (diseases) (use 161)
199 Other scientific research activities

Business and Professional Organizations

200 Business promotion (chamber of commerce, business league, etc.)
201 Real estate association
202 Board of trade
203 Regulating business
204 Promotion of fair business practices
205 Professional association
206 Professional association auxiliary
207 Industry trade shows
208 Convention displays
--- Testing products for public safety (use 905)
209 Research, development, and testing
210 Professional athletic league
--- Attracting new industry (use 403)
--- Publishing activities (use 120)
--- Insurance or other benefits for members (see Employee or Membership Benefit Organizations)
211 Underwriting municipal insurance
212 Assigned risk insurance activities
213 Tourist bureau
229 Other business or professional group

Farming and Related Activities

230 Farming
231 Farm bureau
232 Agricultural group
233 Horticultural group
234 Farmers cooperative marketing or purchasing
235 Financing crop operations
--- FFA, FHA, 4-H club, etc. (use 322)
--- Fair (use 065)
236 Dairy herd improvement association
237 Breeders association
249 Other farming and related activities

Mutual Organizations

250 Mutual ditch, irrigation, telephone, electric company, or like organization
251 Credit union
252 Reserve funds or insurance for domestic building and loan association, cooperative bank, or mutual savings bank
253 Mutual insurance company
254 Corporation organized under an Act of Congress (see also 904)
--- Farmers cooperative marketing or purchasing (use 234)
--- Cooperative hospital service organization (use 157)
259 Other mutual organization

Employee or Membership Benefit Organizations

260 Fraternal beneficiary society, order, or association
261 Improvement of conditions of workers
262 Association of municipal employees
263 Association of employees
264 Employee or member welfare association
265 Sick, accident, death, or similar benefits
266 Strike benefits
267 Unemployment benefits
268 Pension or retirement benefits
269 Vacation benefits
279 Other services or benefits to members or employees

Sports, Athletic, Recreational, and Social Activities

280 Country club
281 Hobby club
282 Dinner club
283 Variety club
284 Dog club
285 Women's club
--- Garden club (use 356)
286 Hunting or fishing club
287 Swimming or tennis club
288 Other sports club
--- Boys Club, Little League, etc. (use 321)
296 Community center
297 Community recreational facilities (park, playground, etc.)
298 Training in sports
299 Travel tours
300 Amateur athletic association
--- School or college athletic association (use 038)
301 Fundraising athletic or sports event
317 Other sports or athletic activities
318 Other recreational activities
319 Other social activities

Youth Activities

320 Boy Scouts, Girl Scouts, etc.
321 Boys Club, Little League, etc.

Code

322 FFA, FHA, 4-H club, etc.
323 Key club
324 YMCA, YWCA, YMHA, etc.
325 Camp
326 Care and housing of children (orphanage, etc.)
327 Prevention of cruelty to children
328 Combat juvenile delinquency
349 Other youth organization or activities

Conservation, Environmental, and Beautification Activities

350 Preservation of natural resources (conservation)
351 Combating or preventing pollution (air, water, etc.)
352 Land acquisition for preservation
353 Soil or water conservation
354 Preservation of scenic beauty
--- Litigation (see Litigation and Legal Aid Activities)
--- Combat community deterioration (use 402)
355 Wildlife sanctuary or refuge
356 Garden club
379 Other conservation, environmental, or beautification activities

Housing Activities

380 Low-income housing
381 Low and moderate income housing
382 Housing for the aged (see also 153)
--- Nursing or convalescent home (use 152)
--- Student housing (use 042)
--- Orphanage (use 326)
398 Instruction and guidance on housing
399 Other housing activities

Inner City or Community Activities

400 Area development, redevelopment, or renewal
--- Housing (see Housing Activities)
401 Homeowners association
402 Other activity aimed at combating community deterioration
403 Attracting new industry or retaining industry in an area
404 Community promotion
--- Community recreational facility (use 297)
--- Community center (use 296)
405 Loans or grants for minority businesses
--- Job training, counseling, or assistance (use 566)
--- Day care center (use 574)
--- Referral service (social agencies) (use 569)
--- Legal aid to indigents (use 462)
406 Crime prevention
407 Voluntary firemen's organization or auxiliary
--- Rescue squad (use 158)
408 Community service organization
429 Other inner city or community benefit activities

Civil Rights Activities

430 Defense of human and civil rights
431 Elimination of prejudice and discrimination (race, religion, sex, national origin, etc.)
432 Lessen neighborhood tensions
449 Other civil rights activities

Litigation and Legal Aid Activities

460 Public interest litigation activities
461 Other litigation or support of litigation
462 Legal aid to indigents
463 Providing bail

Legislative and Political Activities

480 Propose, support, or oppose legislation
481 Voter information on issues or candidates
482 Voter education (mechanics of registering, voting, etc.)
483 Support, oppose, or rate political candidates
484 Provide facilities or services for political campaign activities
509 Other legislative and political activities

Advocacy

Attempt to influence public opinion concerning:
510 Firearms control
511 Selective Service System
512 National defense policy
513 Weapons systems
514 Government spending
515 Taxes or tax exemption
516 Separation of church and state
517 Government aid to parochial schools
518 U.S. foreign policy
519 U.S. military involvement

Code

520 Pacifism and peace
521 Economic-political system of U.S.
522 Anti-communism
523 Right to work
524 Zoning or rezoning
525 Location of highway or transportation system
526 Rights of criminal defendants
527 Capital punishment
528 Stricter law enforcement
529 Ecology or conservation
530 Protection of consumer interests
531 Medical care service
532 Welfare system
533 Urban renewal
534 Busing students to achieve racial balance
535 Racial integration
536 Use of intoxicating beverages
537 Use of drugs or narcotics
538 Use of tobacco
539 Prohibition of erotica
540 Sex education in public schools
541 Population control
542 Birth control methods
543 Legalized abortion
559 Other matters

Other Activities Directed to Individuals

560 Supplying money, goods, or services to the poor
561 Gifts or grants to individuals (other than scholarships)
--- Scholarships for children of employees (use 039)
--- Scholarships (other) (use 040)
--- Student loans (use 041)
562 Other loans to individuals
563 Marriage counseling
564 Family planning
565 Credit counseling and assistance
566 Job training, counseling, or assistance
567 Draft counseling
568 Vocational counseling
569 Referral service (social agencies)
572 Rehabilitating convicts or ex-convicts
573 Rehabilitating alcoholics, drug abusers, compulsive gamblers, etc.
574 Day care center
575 Services for the aged (see also 153 and 382)
--- Training of or aid to the handicapped (see 031 and 160)

Activities Directed to Other Organizations

600 Community Chest, United Way, etc.
601 Booster club
602 Gifts, grants, or loans to other organizations
603 Nonfinancial services or facilities to other organizations

Other Purposes and Activities

900 Cemetery or burial activities
901 Perpetual care fund (cemetery, columbarium, etc.)
902 Emergency or disaster aid fund
903 Community trust or component
904 Government instrumentality or agency (see also 254)
905 Testing products for public safety
906 Consumer interest group
907 Veterans activities
908 Patriotic activities
909 4947(a)(1) trust
910 Domestic organization with activities outside U.S.
911 Foreign organization
912 Title holding corporation
913 Prevention of cruelty to animals
914 Achievement prizes or awards
915 Erection or maintenance of public building or works
916 Cafeteria, restaurant, snack bar, food services, etc.
917 Thrift shop, retail outlet, etc.
918 Book, gift, or supply store
919 Advertising
920 Association of employees
921 Loans or credit reporting
922 Endowment fund or financial services
923 Indians (tribes, cultures, etc.)
924 Traffic or tariff bureau
925 Section 501(c)(1) with 50% deductibility
926 Government instrumentality other than section 501(c)
927 Fundraising
928 4947(a)(2) trust
931 Withdrawal liability payment fund
990 Section 501(k) child care organization